Power Up
Strategies women can use to make a difference in churches

by
Carolyn A. Roth

Power Up: Strategies women can use to make a difference in churches.

Copyright © 2025 by Dr. Carolyn A. Roth. All rights reserved.

No part of the publication may be reproduced, stored in a retrieval system, or transmitted in any way by any means, electronic, mechanical, photocopy, recording, or otherwise, without the prior written permission of the author, except as provided by USA copyright law.

The Bible text used in this edition of the Life Application Study Bible is the Holy Bible, New Living Translation, copyright©1996. 2004, 2015 by Tyndale House Foundation. All rights reserved.

ISBN: 978-1-946919-18-2

Religion & Spirituality>Christian Books & Bibles>Church Leadership>Church Growth
Self Help>Communication & Social Skills
Religion & Spirituality>Religious Studies>Ethics

Dedication

*Frances and Kathryn,
super girlfriends*

Acknowledgements

Bruce Roth (my husband) for editing.
My church

Content

Ch	Title	Page
	Starting Out	9
1	Women in Churches	11
2	Church Power Ethics	21
3	Power Model for Churches	31
4	Expression in Church	37
5	Personal Power Sources	51
6	Roles and Resources	69
7	Known and Knowing	83
8	Willpower in You	99
9	Evaluating Your Power	111
10	Influence in Church	121
11	Positive Influence Tactics	131
12	Negative Manoeuvres	147
	Ending Up	158
	References	161
	Models and Tables	163
	About the Author	165
	Another Read – Level Up	167

Starting Out

Women contribute to almost every aspect of their church. Often, the senior pastor is a man, but women get things done in the church. Women head children's programs, organize fellowship meals, set up communion, and lead many Bible studies.

In Bible times, women were men's property, but they were far from powerless. Present-day Christian women in westernized countries are neither property nor powerless. 21st-century women have the same power sources as 21st-century men.

Interestingly, sources of power haven't changed from Bible times to the present day. What has changed is the way women can and do use their power. They can use their power subtly, as many Bible women used theirs, or they can forthrightly use their power. My concern is that women aren't aware of their potential power and consequently don't use it to better their churches.

The book has three main purposes:

1) To make women aware of their sources of power and influence.

2) To review how and when Bible women used their power. Honestly, in most cases, nothing dire happened.

3) To show how a Christian woman can use power strategies to be phenomenally successful in the church.

Written as a reflective Bible study, *Power Up* stimulates women's self-awareness and teaches them strategies for using power and influence in churches. Consider using it with a group of your church friends to continue your church's success.

Chapter 1

Women in Churches

The greatest impact on women's equality and power in the Western world is Christianity, the largest religion in the world. The Bible, Christian holy scripture, is the best-selling book in the world. In the Bible, women are underrepresented, suggesting a lesser role for women in the Judeo-Christian faith. Nevertheless, women in Christian church leadership are one of the top three issues studied in the 21st century.

There is a resurgence of men attending Christian churches. Men are stepping up, and women are stepping back. Citing dissatisfaction with traditional norms and gender roles, younger women leave the church at higher rates than men.[1] Young women say they don't feel connected to other church congregants, and church teachings don't meet their needs.

About 33% of the United States (U.S.) Christian church pastors are female, while 13% of churches are led (senior pastor) by women. Many women-led churches tended to be smaller in size. Generally, when a woman is ordained, a church hires her as a children's or youth pastor. Some denominations are more open to women as senior pastors, while other denominations view women in the pulpit with less enthusiasm.[2] Surprisingly, younger male pastors are less open to females in the pastorate than older male pastors.

Often, church norms mimic societal norms. Although married households remain the norm in the U.S., in 2023, single-mother families made up 1 in 5 families with children under age 18.[3] Churches must have focused plans to enfold women heads of households in the church. In the 21st-century U.S., few women will engage in a church unless they are fully accepted and empowered in it.

Less than 15% of named characters in the Bible are women. Often, a woman was designated by her hometown, tribe, or male relative, such as her father or husband. Did you notice that although women birthed children, the Bible traced family lineage through males?

Women exploring the Christian faith ask. "Why would I want to be a Christian? The God of the Bible doesn't value women. Weren't Bible women a bunch of chattels?" If chattel is defined as property, then most Bible women were chattels. Ancient cultures viewed women as property of fathers, husbands, and later of sons. A closer read of the Bible shows that although most Bible women were property, they weren't necessarily powerless. In fact, present-day women can use the behavior of biblical women to enhance their power in the church.

In Western churches, women have diverse opinions about women's roles in Christian churches. Where did these differences originate? One answer is traditional views in the Bible on the creation of male and female and the origin of sin. In Christianity, a woman's power evolution goes back to the origins of the Judeo-Christian religion, recorded in Genesis, the first book in the Bible.

In the Bible, there are two creation stories (Genesis chapters 1 and 2). In both, God created two genders, male and female. Both genders were God's image bearers. In neither account did God assign headship to the male or the female. God created both genders for specific purposes—the male (Adam) to tend their garden home and have dominion over all living creatures. The female (Eve) was to act as Adam's helpmeet (helpmate) and to relieve his loneliness.

In 21st-century society, "Helper" is viewed as less than the person being helped. We translate "helper" as assistant, yet that isn't God's perspective. Throughout the Old Testament, God is referenced as the Helper of humankind. In the New Testament, Jesus referred to the Holy Spirit as the Helper, Comforter, and Advocate. Clearly, God the Holy Spirit as a Helper isn't a secondary role. Nor was the female God created secondary or less powerful than the created male.

Despite the clarity in Genesis on the equality (egalitarianism) of males and females, egalitarianism didn't remain after Adam and Eve sinned and were expelled from their garden home. In both the Old and New Testaments and in the Judeo-Christian faith, gender inequality gained traction and persists millennia later.

Power differences between God's image bearers were first recorded in Genesis chapter 3. In the form of a serpent, Satan came to Adam and Eve. Satan tempted them through deception to disobey a direct command from God and eat fruit that their creator prohibited them from eating.

Satan's temptation focused on the fruit's appearance and taste, plus giving the eater as much wisdom as God. Likely, Adam and Eve didn't care too much about another food source, even one that looked good; however, they wanted to be as wise as God. Do you identify with this motive? Many women want to view themselves as wise and to be viewed by others as wise.

Eve took fruit from the Tree of Knowledge of Good and Evil, ate it, and gave some to Adam, who was with her. Adam ate the fruit. The Judeo-Christian religion named Adam and Eve's rebellion against God "sin." After disobeying God, Adam and Eve's eyes were opened. They knew right from wrong; their longed-for goal was achieved.

When God questioned Adam about his rebellion. Adam blamed Eve. Eve blamed the Serpent (Satan). Satan blamed no one—he remained silent. Satan knew his guilt. Do you wonder if Satan was internally gloating that he enticed Adam and Eve, God's acme creation, to disobey God?

Neither Adam nor Eve took personal responsibility for their actions; nonetheless, God assigned responsibility to them. God started with the Serpent, moved to Eve, and ended with Adam (Genesis 3:15-19).

- Serpent/Satan: I will put enmity (deep-seated hatred) between you and the woman and her offspring. Her offspring will crush your head.

- Woman: You will desire your husband. You will have pain in childbirth. Your husband will rule over you.

- Man: The ground will produce corrupt plants. You will toil on the ground for food. You will die.

This specific progression of God's punishment could have no meaning. The order of assignment of punishment could mean that Adam was the least guilty of the three. The order could reflect the entities' power, with the most powerful assigned the most responsibility. Satan was the most powerful being in the triad; he received his discipline first. God decreed Eve's discipline second, suggesting she could have been the second most powerful entity in Eden and/or involved in the rebellion against God. Adam received his discipline last, suggesting he was the least powerful/influential entity in Eden and/or the least culpable creation in the rebellion.

Notice the specific punishment and how it relates to power. Eve's offspring was going to crush Satan's head. Her offspring would destroy Satan. Adam was going to rule over Eve. All of Adam's punishments were solitary. Perhaps, this display acknowledges Adam's loneliness and need for a helpmate.

Through time, through history, Eve was blamed for the fall of humankind. God's stated consequences to Adam and Eve evolved into a hierarchy in their relationship. The male ruled over the woman. The woman became the man's property. As Adam gave names to animals, he gave a name to his wife (Genesis 3:20). Adam had dominion over Eve as he had dominion over animals.

Adam and Eve's sin led to patriarchy. Patriarchy is a social system where dominance and privilege are held by men. Women are relegated to a position below men. Patriarchy promotes prejudice against women (misogyny). Patriarchy and misogyny are reflected in art, literature, human societal structure, historical events, mythology, philosophy, and religion. The male is the power figure who rules over the female.

Although traditional Judeo-Christian belief is patriarchal, there is another base for patriarchy—male physical strength. Most males have more muscle mass than females; consequently, they are physically stronger than women. Physically stronger men were better hunters, farmers, and fighters; thus, they had more power in society. Women wanted to associate with a strong man. A woman wanted a physically strong man for her mate.

Over centuries, what is defined and valued as power has changed. In the 1600s, the Enlightenment Era began and progressed into the Industrial and Technology revolutions. In these eras, physical strength diminished as a reason for power; yet societal views of power changed only minimally. Further, the Judeo-Christian perspective of women being subservient to men, because Eve was deceived by the Serpent, persists in Western Christian churches.

As knowledge and reason became more valued in society, women's power increased. In a technology-driven society, physical strength isn't as important as in previous eras. Still, archaic views of power remain. In the 2005 dictionary, the number one definition of strong is "having greater physical power." Note the word "physical."

Approximately 21 centuries ago, the Son of God (Jesus) came to Earth, born of a woman (Matthew 1:1-25). Through his life, death, and resurrection, the woman's son crushed the head of Satan. The relationship between humankind and God was restored.

> For you are all children of God through faith in Christ Jesus. And all who have been united with Christ in baptism have put on Christ, like putting on new clothes. There is no longer Jew or Gentile, slave or free, male or female. For you are all one in Christ Jesus (Galatians 3:26-29).

Jesus' death was meant to restore humankind's relationship with God.

Unfortunately, the balance of power—gender equity—between men and women wasn't restored. Thus, we come to Complementarianism, a religious perspective on the roles of males and females in the Christian church. Complementarity teaches God-ordained complementary roles for males and females. Men and women are equal but different. A clear example is that just as a man can't birth a child, a woman shouldn't *(can't)* lead a church, including preach a sermon.

The much-loved Christian missionary, Paul, wrote that women were to be subject to their husbands, silent in the church, and ask their husbands what they want to know about spiritual matters (1 Timothy 2:11-15). To support his position, Paul noted that Eve led Adam to rebel against God; thus, Eve is the weaker link in the male-female dyad.

Final Thoughts

Citing dissatisfaction with traditional norms and gender roles, younger women leave the church at higher rates than men.[1] Young women say they don't feel connected to other church congregants, and church teaching doesn't meet their needs.

In 21st-century churches, disagreements about women's roles in churches abound between men and women and among women. Women aren't unified on their perspective about women's roles in the church. In recent decades, I've attended several evangelical churches. In one denomination, bylaws averred that women could be pastors. Yet, no women were ordained in that church. A woman church friend vehemently declared that women should be silent in the church; men should lead the church, including preaching sermons.

One church, founded on the doctrine of equality, had a five-member elected Leadership Committee. The Committee was the decision-making body for the church. All were men despite church membership being majority female. I approached the senior pastor about the lack of women on the Leadership Committee. He responded that the Praise Team (singers) contained more women than men. Seemingly, my message wasn't heard and/or accepted.

Society has no reason to conclude that gender and power evolution are over. Sound arguments continue for changes in gender power dynamics. First, the number of jobs that don't require physical strength is increasing.

Men with physical strength aren't needed to fill these jobs, i.e., medicine, academe, politics, and business. Women are claiming them.

Second, biologically, fewer men than women are needed to populate the Earth. A healthy male releases 40 million to 1.2 billion sperm cells (XY chromosome) in one ejaculation. In contrast, women produce one egg cell (XX chromosome) with each monthly fertility cycle. One male can fertilize hundreds of female eggs and maintain the population of Earth. In future centuries, will men become superfluous?

Points to Ponder

Why purchase a book about Christian women's power in churches? What do you expect to learn/get from this book?

How satisfied are you with the roles of women in Old Testament times? What would have made their roles better?

How satisfied are you with the role you have in your church? What would make your roles better?

When did you last conclude that meeting one of your church's needs "isn't your job?"

Which model, egalitarianism, patriarchy, or complementarity, resonates with you? Why? Which one(s) don't you like? Why?

Chapter 2

Church Power Ethics

Gender equity in a church can be a threat to some individuals, both men and women. The rationale goes something like this: Eve led Adam into sin. If women are in positions of power, they may lead the church into sin. For this reason, many Christians snub women in power positions in the church, and they snub men who speak about gender equity. My husband walked into a men's Bible study. The leader said, "Here comes the women's libber." That happened about 12 years ago; my husband remembers what happened and remains hurt by the comment.

As Christian women, ideally, we claim our church power, not through "in your face" dominance tactics. Christian women can become powerful in churches using the fruit of the Spirit, love, joy, peace, patience, kindness, goodness, and faithfulness (Galatians 5:22-23).

God's Perspective on Power

Two verses in the Bible summarize God's perspective on power. They give guidelines for women seeking and using power. First, power belongs to God:

> God has spoken plainly, and I have heard it many times: Power, O God, belongs to you; (Psalm 62:11).

Nothing on Earth occurs, be it a cataclysmic event, a queen crowned, or a flower dropping a petal, unless God wills it. All that happens under, on, and above Earth is according to God's plan. God allows a woman to use her power to influence others; nevertheless, God can override a woman's power.

The second Bible verse about power is an instruction to individuals with power in the church. It directs individuals on how they should act:

> Do not withhold good from those to
> whom it is due, when it is in your power
> to act (Proverbs 3:27).

Read the following seven instructive Bible verses on power. Notice, none of these verses that promise power through Jesus is given to men only. The promises are given to Christian believers regardless of gender. The verses tell us how we should behave.

- For he (Jesus) lives by the power of God. We will live with him by the power of God (2 Corinthians 13:4).

- For the kingdom of God does not consist in talk but in power (1 Corinthians 4:20).

- God gave us a spirit not of fear but of power and love and self-control (2 Timothy 1:7-8).

- His (Jesus') divine power has granted to us all things that pertain to life and godliness (2 Peter 1:3).

- They who wait for the Lord shall renew their

strength. They shall run and not be weary; they shall walk and not faint (Isaiah 40:30-31).

- I can do all things through him (Jesus) who strengthens me (Philippians 4:13).

- My grace is sufficient for you, for my power is made perfect in weakness (2 Corinthians 12:9).

How to Use Power

One definition of power is the ability to act in a particular way. Women have power over themselves. Women can opt not to go to Sunday church services or Bible study. Women can get a cup of coffee or tea. Power gives women the ability to direct or influence another's behavior. Women can persuade, cajole, and coerce other individuals in your church.

Power tinges every human interaction. Powerful and powerless individuals live side-by-side in society, but in different worlds. Men and women worship side-by-side in church, but often see the church differently. Ponder that male Bible writers included little information on women, possibly because they didn't understand women. Possibly, men in churches don't see women's activities and power because they don't understand them.

Women who view themselves as less powerful than men in church experience more negative emotions, are more alert to threats than to rewards, and act in more inhibited ways. In contrast, individuals who feel powerful:

- Feel free to be themselves.

- Remain consistent in the way they describe

themselves.

- Are comfortable sharing opinions.

- Are goal-oriented but willing to work harder toward achieving objectives.

- They are likely to act rather than take no action toward goals.

An American proverb is "power corrupts." Many women heard that comment so often growing up that it became a permanent belief even into adulthood. Several years ago, I sat in a classroom listening to a lively discussion on power. One student asked the professor whether or not he believed the proverb that "Power corrupts, and absolute power corrupts absolutely".

In class discussions, students concluded that power is neither moral nor immoral. Power is amoral. The way an individual uses power determines its morality. Power can lead to temptation to abuse it, but individuals don't have to abuse power. Power doesn't have to corrupt a male or female's behavior in society at large or in church.

Should Christian women avoid or back away from power because it can corrupt them? Probably not. Most examples of Bible women showed that they used their power to benefit others, but sometimes they used it to harm others. We agree that Jezebel used her power as King Ahab's wife to threaten and kill individuals. Herodias used power over her daughter to obtain the head of John the Baptist.

Occasionally, a woman's power got the opposite of what

she wanted. Eve's reason for eating the forbidden fruit was her desire for knowledge; that's laudable. Unfortunately, Eve's action contributed to her and Adam

being kicked out of their garden home because she disobeyed her creator and led Adam to disobey God.

Ethical Use of Power

Brett Beasley[4] identified four ways to use power ethically. Christian women can use these strategies in their churches.

Be Responsible: Focus on the responsibility that comes with power. How should women with power behave? Last evening I attended my church's midweek Bible study. Our teacher was a 50-something woman pastor. Clearly, she had power in the group; however, she presented herself as a learner, the same as the rest of us. She was attractive, warm, and open. She did her homework on the topic; she had notes and showed a video. She had good group leadership skills, encouraging input from each group member. I'm going back next week.

Have Morals: Develop a strong moral identity. Women with good moral identity—who have values, act justly, and are caring and generous—are less likely to act out of self-interest when in powerful positions. Further, women in tight-knit communities (such as churches) are often willing to share rather than hoard power. Think back on what you know of women's lives in biblical times. There was a communal lifestyle among them. They shared rather than hoarded.

During our marriage, my husband and I attended a large (think mega) church. We also attended a small community church with Sunday attendance of around 60. Most U.S. churches are relatively small. In a smaller church, a woman is known. Other congregants know what she values and what she doesn't value. They know if she is there for power or there to serve.

Speak Up: When there is a problem, encourage others to speak up and act (even when that problem is you). Women who feel powerless speak up less, whether in a mixed gender group or a women-only group. One of my friends is less vocal than the other two of us. Her opinions and points of view aren't heard as often as ours. Some identify her as less powerful in the triad. That's not accurate. Importantly, power is more related to what a person says than the number of times a woman speaks. Nonetheless, ethical leaders want all group members to have equal opportunity to speak and act. Ethical leaders collaborate with others, allowing everyone to speak.

Stay Humble: Find mentors who keep you humble. These mentors may be outside your church, where the mentor isn't influenced by a churchwoman's personal power. Do you ever wonder if the young girl Mary felt pride after Gabriel announced that she would conceive and bear the Son of God? A clue to the answer is in Mary's Magnificat (Luke 1:6-55). Mary claimed that future generations would call her blessed. This comment suggested that young Mary could have felt pride, be it minuscule, at being chosen as the Messiah's earthly mother. Possibly, Mary used Elizabeth as an external mentor. Elizabeth lived 80-100 miles, and a 4-5 day walk from Mary's home in Nazareth.

Ethical use of power isn't easy
even in church.

Ethics for Congregants

The Christian church is embodied in local congregations. The National Association of Evangelicals[5] published Codes of Ethics for church leaders and congregants that include women. Although there are different codes of ethics published by different groups, almost all encompass six points:

1) Honor and support the gifts Jesus gave churches. Gifts include apostles, prophets, evangelists, pastors, and teachers.

2) Promote the unity of the body of Jesus. There is one body, one Spirit, and one hope for the future.

3) Practice accountability. Model openness and clear communication in doing the congregation's business.

4) Practice good stewardship. Use gifts as they are intended. Honor financial record-keeping. Report practices to the membership and denominational networks.

5) Practice hospitality. As each has received a gift, use it to serve one another.

6) Seek the welfare of the community where God has placed the church.

Final Thoughts

It's not always easy to act ethically. Sometimes women think that an action is ethical, but when the act is viewed from outside the situation, it is questionable.

In my hometown, a young man was denied entry into a seminary. His bishop, a woman, refused to give him a recommendation. She wanted to increase the number of women in the pastorate and was only recommending women to the local seminary. The bishop's action may have been unethical despite her good intentions.

The story had a semi-happy ending—the young man was admitted to another denomination's seminary. The downside was that his denomination lost a godly pastor. Another downside is that the story of his woman bishop's failure to recommend him to the denomination's seminary is widely known. Both men and women see a sample of reverse gender discrimination in her action.

Points to Ponder

Do you ever get jealous when you see an influential, successful woman in your church? What do you do?

One Bible verse about power is, "For the kingdom of God does not consist in talk but in power" (1 Corinthians 4:20). What does that verse mean? How does it apply to your conduct in church?

Have you ever feared that you would be corrupted by power, that is, you would become arrogant, prideful, or some other negative attribute?

Would an individual in your community conclude you are a Christian by the way you use power?

Have you seen power brokers among church leaders? What did they do? Did they act ethically? If you answered no, compare their behavior with the six ethics for congregants.

Chapter 3

Power Model for Churches

As I investigated Christian women's power and opportunities in churches, I kept turning back to Dr. Terry Bacon's[6] gender-neutral power model. Gender neutral means both men and women use the same types of power. In Bacon's model, there's no such thing as male and female power; there's only power.

Bacon[6] identified two power categories: personal and positional. Personal power is the traits and characteristics of a person. In contrast, positional power is tied to relationships with others, i.e., a job title or a significant other.

Diagram of Bacon's Model of Power[6]

Bible women used personal power and positional power to get what they wanted and get things done. Biblical women had goals separate from men. They knew that if they wanted to be effective in their environments, whether that environment was a home, harem, tribe, or kingdom, they had to both have and use power. Today, the churchwomen have goals separate from men. Using their personal and positional power, they got things done.

Both the Bible and 21st-century women understand that their power begins with themselves; it's personal. Personal power has five aspects: a woman's way of expressing herself; her knowledge, character, and attraction; and her history or relationship with the other person(s).

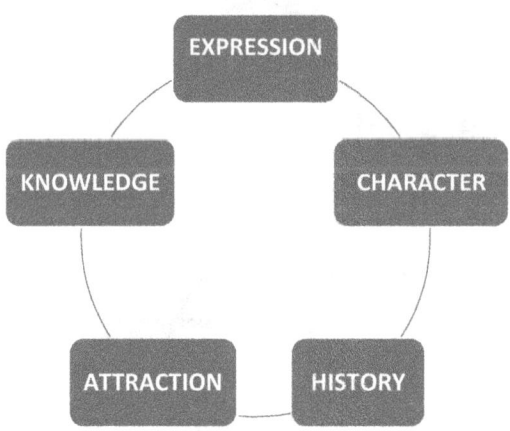

Sources of Personal Power[6]

In Bacon's[6] gender-neutral power model, the second source of power is position. At one time, i.e., in the Bible, a woman's positional power was related to a man or men in her life. Was she the wife of the king or of a successful, wealthy man? In the 21st century, women have additional positional power sources. Some own a business or are high in the corporate ladder. Some control wealth. Some have their own wealth.

Position power encompasses 1) the roles a woman occupies, 2) resources she controls, 3) her reputation, 4) the information a woman has or has access to, and 5) networks she has with others.

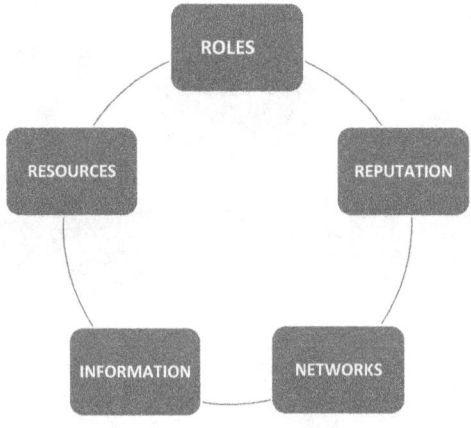

Sources of Positional Power[6]

When describing role and resource position power, I place them in the same chapter (Chapter 4) because they are so closely aligned. Chapter 5 includes a discussion of reputation, information, and network power, again because these three are so closely aligned.

Deciding whether personal or positional power is more important is hard. The answer depends on the situation and perhaps the values in the church.

Management guru Terry Bacon[6] claimed that will power magnifies every other (personal and positional) power source. According to Walt Whitman, character and willpower were the only investments worth making.

Willpower is a mega source of power

From Bacon's perspective, willpower is composed of a woman's beliefs, desires, and motives.

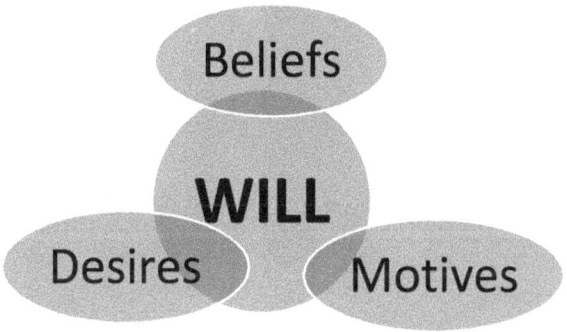

Sources of Willpower[6]

Final Thoughts

Think about it: finally, a power perspective (a model):

- That isn't different for men and women.

- Unconnected to the time of the culture or society.

- Not specific to location, i.e., family, church, corporations, government.

That's the power model that will be used to discuss the actions of historic Judeo-Christian women. That's the power model advocated for Christian church women in this book.

Points to Ponder

Do you believe that power is the same in both men and women? Why or why not?

Is it logical for the same characteristics of power to be present over millennia, or do power characteristics change over time? Explain your answer.

Is power the same whether it occurs in a family, church, or nation?

Identify other aspects of personal and positional power to add to Bacon's model.

Willpower is composed of beliefs, desires, and motives. How do these components relate to a woman's personality?

Chapter 4

Expression in Church

Chapter 4 focuses on how a woman expresses herself, a type of personal power. It includes dos and don'ts if women want to be eloquent in church and elsewhere. Expressiveness is a woman's ability to communicate powerfully and effectively.

> *Expression gives more clout than any other personal power[6]*

Women are natural expressers, primarily expressing themselves in words. Ruth was an Old Testament woman with expressive word power. Arguably, Ruth was the most eloquent woman in the Bible. Here's the story of Ruth and her expression.

Naomi, an Israelite woman along with her husband and two sons, relocated to Moab because of a famine in the Bethlehem region. While in Moab, Naomi's sons married Moabite women, Ruth and Orpah. Then, Naomi's husband and sons died. Naomi decided to return to Bethlehem. She directed her daughters-in-law to return to their Moabite families. Ruth refused to leave Naomi. Ruth's words to Naomi were:

> Don't urge me to leave you or to turn back from you. Where you go I will go, and where you stay I will stay. Your people will be my people and your God my God. Where you die I will die, and there I will be buried. May the Lord deal with me, be it ever so severely, if even death separates you and me (Ruth 1:16-17).

Powerful expressions, such as those Ruth used and that 21st-century church women use, have three requirements: they are substantive, concise, and correct. As you read about these three characteristics, ask yourself if you express yourself like Ruth:

- Substantive means that the words are relevant to the topic and move the line of thought forward. Ruth's comment made it clear she wasn't leaving Naomi despite Naomi's direction. Ruth's words essentially ended the conversation between herself and Naomi.

- In her response to Naomi, Ruth used no empty words, no fillers, and perhaps no verbal pauses. Ruth knew what she planned to say and expressed herself succinctly.

- When we read Ruth's statement, word selection, sentence structure, and grammar seem ideal.

The human brain loves patterns and repetitions. When women use word patterns and repetitions, what they say is remembered. Ruth's words to Naomi flowed because of word repetition, i.e., you go, I go; you stay, I stay; your God, my God. Today, Ruth's words are memorized and repeated in wedding vows. They resonated with us who have loved another person and wanted to be with that person. I believe that the 66 words in *Ruth* were a reason the *Book of Ruth* was included in the canon of Scripture.

Crafting Messages

I once worked with a woman who had great ideas—if I listened to her long enough. She spoke countless words before she got to the point of her message. Some individuals tuned her out altogether. Although this incident happened in a work environment, it happens in churches. Get to the point of your message.

In the 21st century, some women take little time to think out a message before they start to speak. Rarely do they ask themselves, "What is the best way to convey my perspective on the situation?" They open their mouths and spew forth words, only thinking out their message as they talk. That isn't eloquence; that isn't expressive power. Slowing down gives space to think and clarify what we want to express. Once clarified, we can better articulate our message and show expression power.

In text messages and emails, women abbreviate thoughts. My associate pastor's preferred method of communicating is text messages. When I communicate with him in a text message, much of what I want to say doesn't get included. I can't seem to get all my thoughts in the text message. Plus, the letter keys are small. Perhaps after all, text messages are good because women must focus on what is important to communicate.

Sometimes women zip off emails or text messages when frustrated or angry. They write what they would never say when calm. Impulsive communication isn't a good idea in church or other environments. Pause, Breathe, Think!

In the New Testament, a woman showed that a woman's wordcraft remained over centuries, and women who communicate effectively fill their speech with images and metaphors that create pictures in listeners' minds. Jesus went to the Gentile area of Tyre and Sidon. Jesus wanted to rest. He didn't want anyone to know he was there. A local woman learned that Jesus was in town. She went to the house where he stayed. She begged Jesus to heal her daughter, who was possessed by a demon.

Initially, Jesus refused to heal the daughter, saying that it wasn't right to take children's bread and toss it to dogs. The woman's rebuttal was, "Even the dogs under the table eat the children's crumbs" (Mark 7:28). This Gentile woman created a masterful word picture. We see children sitting at a kitchen table eating lunch. Being children, they drop food on the floor. Under the table, opportunistic dogs snap up dropped food. Jesus told the woman that because of her reply, her daughter was healed.

Expressive Silence

Women can show expressive power through silence. Unfortunately, Bible readers can't be sure when Bible women used silence as a personal power strategy versus when Bible recorders omitted women's words. Rarely, if ever, do we read, "After a thoughtful pause, the woman said............"

In the 21st century, women in church should learn the skill of verbal expression at times and of silence at other times. Advice on silence is embedded in an American proverb, "Silence speaks louder than words." Psychologists name this type of silence as the "response of non-responding." At times, non-responding is deafening.

Not too long ago, I sent an email to my pastor asking him a question. After several months with no response, I sent a follow-up email asking if he had received my original email and had input for me. No response to my second email came back. Granted, I live in the South, where sometimes silence is an avoidance tactic and means "No," nevertheless, I was left hanging. What was his answer? I assumed his answer was "No," but I could have been wrong, after all, an American proverb is "Silence is consent". I wanted an answer! My church's Prayer of Confession on Sunday included, "We have spoken without an effort to understand others. We have kept silent instead of telling the truth."

The American proverb "Silence is consent" has been around a long time. Yet, church women know that their silence doesn't always mean they consent to what is said or decided. Sometimes, silence means you disagree but don't want to draw attention to yourself. At other times, the issue doesn't matter to you.

Women ask themselves what they want their silence to mean, i.e., agreement, acceptance, or resentment? Whatever they expect the silence to convey, a woman's silence influences others. Below is advice on the value of silence.[7]

1. Listening builds trust. For trust to develop, a woman must be listened to. When a churchwoman realizes her colleagues are silent and listening to her, she listens to them. She thinks about what they say. Mutual trust is built.

2. Silence can be used to emphasize a point. Silence allows a woman to be heard when it matters. In a church meeting, a woman shouldn't answer every question posed to the group. Rather, she should respond to one or two questions. In that way, her words are more memorable.

The more words, the less attention they get

3. Silence can be nerve-racking. Silence is a negotiation tool. When a woman is silent, listeners wonder what she's thinking. The discomfort of silence makes the listener want to fill the void and start talking. From others' words, you learn information.

4. Silence empowers others. Powerful women rarely tell others what to do. They allow others—even children—to suggest ideas to achieve goals. A much-used saying of management guru, Peter Drucker, was that "Work belongs to the worker." Your silence allows others to be involved in a project's solution.

5. Silence gets answers. The sooner a woman becomes silent, the sooner she gets answers. Many women are guilty of asking a question and then continuing to talk. Continued speech prevents potential responders from answering. This behavior says that listeners' responses aren't important. Have you ever had that happen in a

Bible study or Sunday school class?

A woman's question has more weight and more power if she just stops talking and lets listeners answer the question! Further, never add to a question with excuses. Excuses dilute the question and the power of the message.

6. Take time for silence. A woman who wants power must take time for silence during the day. Silent times are particularly important when a woman is surrounded by children.

Words that Alienate

Today, I attended the first day of a 20-hour course as a volunteer at a pregnancy center. About eight times, during a two-hour lecture, the instructor said "language matters" as she exhorted attendees to use value-free words when talking about the sensitive topic of pregnancy.

A woman's words can enfold or alienate listeners. Words can add or subtract from power. Women in churches need to practice using value-free words, i.e., your child's father rather than your spouse.

Words go in and out of style just as clothes do. A word that is common in one period is unintelligible in another, i.e., "flow on," "lawfare." Plus, words can have a meaning in one church that differs from the meaning in another church. Words can have different meanings in the same church at different times.

Several years ago, I became a committee chairperson in my church. To maximize time and travel (gas prices were high), committee members decided to hold meetings via a computer meeting program. In one meeting, a motion was made. When the discussion was held, a member wrote that she was "concerned" about the motion and listed several reasons. No one, including myself, responded to her "concerns." Other committee members had no concerns. Subsequently, the motion passed.

Later, a church colleague told me that saying, "I'm concerned," was church-speak for "I disagree." A year previously, the church had a consultant who offered ways for church members to be more effective communicators. One way was to not disagree openly with each other. Instead, church members should phrase their disagreement by saying "I'm concerned".

I was clueless about this church convention, so I took no action when the member wrote that she was "concerned." In retrospect, I feel guilty about my non-action. The church member may have concluded that I discounted her perspective. Giving no response to her concern could have alienated her and reduced my power with her. At the same time, her expressive power was reduced by using a phrase with a meaning unknown to all committee members.

Power Draining Words

Words are powerful. Small words and phrases can impact a woman's power. A recently published article identified six verbs a woman shouldn't use if she wants to project power. These verbs are *think, need, want, guess, hope, and suppose.*[8] The article focused on women in the work world; however, these words apply to women who want power in the church.

Think: Most of us have heard the expression, "I think," particularly in church committee meetings. Technically, "think" means that an individual conceives in the mind, then considers or meditates on the topic. Possibly, a pastor does that, but many women don't meditate on a topic or idea before giving their opinion. Beginning a sentence with "I think" is a habit, rather than implying any evaluation. Using "I think" suggests that an individual is still pondering the idea and hasn't reached a firm conclusion.

"I think" rarely influences anyone who hears it. "I think" is an admission that this opinion may be one of many. Women who are trying to influence others should delete the "I think" phrase and proceed directly to the input. In church, instead of saying, "I think that we should have an education series on the Armor of God, a woman could say, "Let's have a course on the Armor of God.

Need: A woman who uses the verb "need" sounds dependent. The woman undercuts her power and her directive. She sounds needy rather than forceful. To sound more confident, a woman can simply convey her message. A woman teaching a Sunday school class can tell the church secretary, "I need 25 copies of this outline for Sunday morning," or "Please have 25 copies of this outline available for me on Sunday morning." The latter sentence is more likely to influence the secretary to do the copying and have it available for Sunday morning.

Want: "Want" is a verb like "need. "Want" suggests the speaker is lacking in some way. I was appointed chairperson of a church committee. I asked the pastor how much money was budgeted for the committee. How much money did the committee have for educational resources, field trips, food, etc. I could have said, I want or need to know….. "Want" and "need" are part of the church vocabulary. It may be difficult to ask a question without using them. Try!

Guess: Saying "I guess" conveys tentativeness. Likely, a woman won't be able to influence anyone if she only "guesses" she can do something or guesses something will occur. The dictionary defines "guess" as forming an opinion, with little or no evidence. The chairperson for the church missionary committee could respond to queries of annual giving with "we are on schedule to have a 10% income over budget expenses this year" rather than say, "I guess we'll meet budget."

Hope: Some women begin statements with "I hope," i.e., "I hope to start the meeting at 7:00 p.m." "I hope you'll be able to take that assignment." "Hope" has a prayer-like quality. In church, "hope" implies that the speaker doesn't know or control the outcome. An alternative to using the word "hope" is "I know you will give the class your all." Notice how empowering that word "know" is.

Suppose: You're having coffee with a church friend. In my church, women get together every Saturday morning at the local coffee shop. No agenda, just to socialize. At one of these get-togethers, another woman asks if you're going to an upcoming church meeting. You answer, "I suppose so." By saying "I suppose," you are saying that you don't care about the meeting one way or another.

"I suppose so" erodes a woman's power!

There are few, if any, church situations where conveying indifference and inertia improves a woman's power. Instead, women should find something to express enthusiasm about (even if it's not the meeting itself). "Yes, I'll be there. I want to hear what the pastor says." Alternatively, if you aren't planning to attend, honestly say so. You don't have to give a reason for the nonattendance. You may not think your response matters, but it does. News travels fast. If your words repeatedly suggest a "don't care" attitude, your power dips.

Regional Differences

The U.S. is a mobile society. More than likely, a woman won't remain all her life in the area or region where she was born. I'm a Yankee; I was born in the northeast. Yet I've lived most of my life in the South, i.e., South Carolina, Texas, and Virginia. Southern women view Northern women's communications as abrupt and brash. They describe Northern women as having no verbal boundaries. Northern women find Southern women's expressions (God love her!) hilarious and their communication style passive-aggressive. Notice, I wrote, passive-aggressive rather than merely aggressive (that's Northern women).

To have expressive power, women must adjust their communications to the region they live in. The region/church congregants won't modify their expressions to the out-of-region woman. When I write "adjust," I'm not suggesting that a woman mimic the accent of another region. That is talking down and reduces a woman's power.

The U.S. is a nation of immigrants. Churches are or should be a diverse community of native English speakers and immigrants with English as a second or third language. When immigrants to the U.S. speak English, they often have accents. This morning, Melania Trump was a guest on "Fox and Friends." She was helping children decorate Christmas trees. Mrs. Trump has a heavy Slovenian accent. So what? Who cares? She was loving and kind.

Christian women must accept accents. We can't act as if individuals are inferior because they speak our language with an accent. Nor can we ignore them or refuse to interact with them.

Final Thoughts

The gap between the influence ratings of a woman with high versus low expressive power was wider than for any other personal power source!!!

Articulate women are more powerful than women who speak in rambling, jumbled sentences. Church women, who want to convince others of the truth of Jesus' gift of salvation, must present Jesus persuasively. Equally, true women who want to convince others of their point of view must create substantial, focused arguments.

Silence while communicating implies the listener is focused on what you are saying. You feel valued.

The words that Humphrey[8] identified as powerless or throw-away words are common in church communication. In fact, they are so common that they seem part of "church speak". Contemplate the message you convey when you use these words.

Points to Ponder

Why are so few women quoted in the Bible in comparison to the number of men? Are women poorer communicators than men?

Do you believe the proverb "silence is golden" is true for Christian women? What does that proverb mean for women's expression of power in the church? Is the proverb accurate there?

Should individuals entering the U.S. be required to learn English, the dominant language of the country? How are English-speaking women in U.S. churches more advantaged than non-English speakers?

Can you name a word or phrase used in your church that could have no meaning in another church?

What does the saying, "What she does speaks so loudly, I can't hear what she says," mean? How does it apply to women's expression of power?

Chapter 5

Personal Power Sources

Although expressive power is the premier personal power source, there are four others: knowledge, character, attraction, and history[6] (sometimes known as the relationship you have with another). Bible women's power was from God. In the 21st century, churchwomen have power from God. The power of all women—in biblical times and in the 21st century—is given for God's glory.

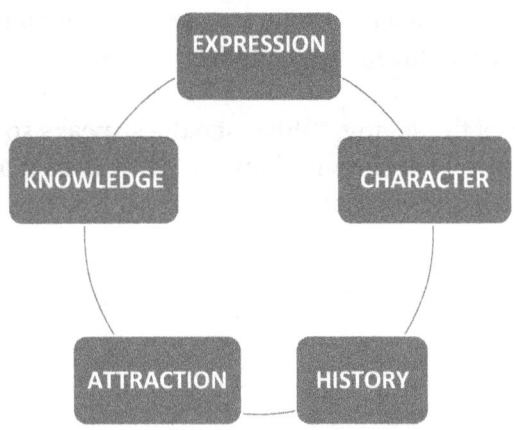

Sources of Personal Power

Knowledge Power

"Knowledge makes you strong" is an American proverb most of us have heard since childhood. My mother used it to get me out of bed for school in the morning. In reality, that proverb is from the Bible, "The wise are mightier than the strong, and those with knowledge grow stronger and stronger" (Proverbs 24:5).

In all ancient cultures, i.e., Israelite, Egyptian, Persian, Roman, writers and rulers recognized that some women were "in the know" while others weren't. The Bible is replete with stories about knowledgeable women. In the 21st century, many women have a distinct knowledge specialty. One friend quilts. Another owns a restaurant and makes the best food. Knowledge isn't only what a person knows. Knowledge encompasses skills, abilities, talents, and accomplishments.

Today, Americans estimate an individual's knowledge by their credentials: PhD, CEO, JD; their title or position: business owner, doctor, professor, senator, prime minister; and various affiliations and honors: Mensa, Oxford, MIT, Nobel Prize, or Olympic Medal. Bible women had none of those designations. Most couldn't read or write; yet their actions proved that they had knowledge and ability, and ultimately, power.

Knowledge alone didn't and doesn't increase a woman's power. When a Bible woman had knowledge, but no one knew about it, her knowledge was irrelevant. The same is true in the 21st century. A woman must share her knowledge to be admired and considered both an expert and "in the know."

Knowledge increases a woman's power only if her knowledge is recognized

When sharing critical information in churches, timing is important. Congregants don't hear a woman's knowledge until it directly affects them. Think about a situation when a woman shares knowledge at a critical moment, i.e., when the knowledge is most needed. Other individuals talk about her contribution. She's respected. When a woman's knowledge is timely, she is more powerful.

One of the best examples of knowledge power in the Old Testament was the Queen Mother in Babylon. Her son, King Belshazzar, gave a banquet. Stunningly, during the banquet, a hand wrote on the banquet room wall! No astrologer, magician, or diviner could decipher the words. Everyone in the room, from king to servant, was in a tizzy.

Finally, the Queen Mother entered the banquet hall. She told King Belshazzar that Daniel, a man brought to Babylon from Judah by her husband (Nebuchadnezzar), could interpret the writing on the banquet wall. Daniel was brought to the banquet hall. Daniel told King Belshazzar what the words said and meant for the Babylonian kingdom.

The Bible didn't record the name of the Queen Mother; however, she had power. Her power was knowledge of Daniel and his ability. Knowledge unknown to Belshazzar's wisest men. We have no record of what happened to this royal woman, but in this time and place, hers was the most powerful voice in the room. Notice the timing of the Queen Mother's input. She waited to share her knowledge until the magicians and wise men admitted that they couldn't interpret the banquet wall writing.

A contemporary church example occurred when a church's Christian Education Committee discussed the education curriculum for the upcoming year. A proposed topic was "Queen Esther." A woman, active in a community Bible study, knew that Queen Esther was taught in that group last year. She shared her knowledge, and as expected, the church eliminated Queen Esther as a curriculum choice because many of the church's women attended community Bible study.

Other Committee members viewed the woman contributor as smart and connected in the community. If the woman said nothing, her knowledge wouldn't benefit the Education Committee. Other Committee members wouldn't see her as knowing.

In addition to not sharing knowledge, another way a woman can diminish her knowledge power in church is by giving wrong or misleading information. This wrong information goes beyond something as minor as quoting a Bible verse in a different Bible translation. It encompasses faking knowledge and then being found out, or not being able to prove an assertion. A woman who does this loses knowledge credibility. Possibly, she will no longer be able to influence others using her knowledge. Others stop acting on, even listening to, what she says.

Another way misuse of knowledge can diminish a woman's power is by having a know-it-all attitude. No person knows it all, not even the most educated and/or well-rounded individual in your congregation. As 2025 news commentators state, "stay in your lane." Don't pretend you know something you don't.

A final action that diminishes a woman's knowledge and power when leading a church group is not knowing the knowledge and skills of the group members she leads. As the group leader, a woman doesn't have to be an expert on every topic discussed. Knowing the expertise of each committee member, the leader can solicit their opinion when needed.

Character Power

A woman's character can add or subtract from every other personal power source, including knowledge.[6] Character is the way a woman typically thinks, feels, behaves, and the mental and moral qualities distinct in her. Character draws others, whether those others are community acquaintances or church friends. Each of us wants to associate with women of good character. We act like, or perhaps hope, their character power rubs off on us.

A woman's character impacts her credibility, i.e., whether others believe what she says. A woman can be knowledgeable, but if she has character flaws, her power is diminished. Character flaws include being defensive, aloof, and volatile. A sense of entitlement, making destructive comments, and self-focus are character flaws. They reduce a 21st-century woman's character power in the church.

While thinking about the Bible woman who showed character power, I remembered the adage, "If you want to know a woman's character, look at her behavior." Then, I considered the character power of Rizpah, Queen Ano, and Abigail. Finally, I settled on Jephthah's daughter as an example of a woman with character power. About now, some of you are shaking your head and saying, "Never heard of her. Who's Jephthah?"

Jephthah was a Judge east of the Jordan River who led the Israelites against the Ammonites. Before a battle, he promised that if God gave him victory, he would sacrifice whatever first exited his home's door. His only child, a daughter, was the first individual out the door. Jephthah was devastated.

Jephthah's daughter could easily have gotten out of being sacrificed. First, she could have reminded her father that human sacrifice was an abomination to God. Second, rather than sacrifice her, Jephthah could "give" her as a living sacrifice to God. As such, she would have remained unmarried throughout her life. Finally, Jephthah's daughter could have tried tearful persuasion to convince Jephthah not to sacrifice her. Jephthah loved his daughter, his only child. He would have tried hard—even risked being forsworn—to find a way out of this terrible predicament. Instead, Jephthah's daughter told her father:

> My father, you have opened your mouth to the Lord; do to me according to what has gone out of your mouth, now that the Lord has avenged you on your enemies, on the Ammonites (Judges 11:36).

Jephthah's daughter dared to hold her father's feet to the fire and insist that he fulfill his vow to God. Perhaps Jephthah's daughter knew something her father didn't, i.e., that a good character is more desirable than great riches. If Jephthah didn't keep his vow to God, he could have lost his credibility as a leader.

Unlike Bible writers who wrote chapters, even books, about the lives of Old Testament women, often New Testament writers recorded only snippets of information about them. One such woman was Anna. Anna was a prophetess from the tribe of Asher. When Luke introduced Anna, she was approximately 84 years old. Anna lived in the Women's Court of the Jerusalem temple, where she fasted and prayed. The Women's Court was about 200 square feet. The average living room in a U.S. home is 200-350 square feet. Imagine living in the small, circumscribed space that Anna lived in for 50 years.

In 21st-century U.S. churches, a good character, i.e., integrity, sincerity, goodness, kindness, may seem irrelevant or outdated. Yet, women should remember that individuals watch them at church. I arrive at church early and watch other congregants. Every Sunday, Justin and Alice snuggle up. Kathy and Perry sat down with four chairs between them so that when their daughter and her family enter, they can all sit together. Teenage girls occupy an entire row of seats. Those girls change their hair color at least once a month. This week it's orange. What a diverse group of Christians!

In the first several decades of the 21st century, more women than men have stopped attending church.[1] Women's absence creates a power and service drain in the church. Just as important, or perhaps more important, than Christian women who stop attending church are the ones who remain as members but engage in the 21st-century phenomena of learned helplessness and quiet quitting. Learned helplessness almost always precedes quiet quitting.

Learned helplessness occurs when a woman believes that nothing she does matters or makes a difference.[9] Consequently, she becomes passive. In church, a woman may see no value or positive outcome for contributing. She comes to believe nothing she does matters. She believes her contributions aren't valued. Her moral qualities make no difference. When a woman views her knowledge and character as having no impact on a church's decisions or activities, she gives up.

Likely, the learned helplessness leads to quietly quitting.[9] "Quiet quitting" is a fairly new phenomenon in churches and evolved from behavior during the Covid-19 epidemic in the U.S. Quiet quitting occurs when individuals attend Sunday service or have their names on membership rolls, but in all other ways are nonparticipants in the church. Recently, more women than men have become quiet quitters. These women stay silent at church meetings, rarely take the initiative to seek out church activities, and engage minimally in solving church problems.

Most of the literature available on quiet quitting is from the business world and was written during and immediately after the COVID-19 epidemic. Gurus identified that the best way to counter quiet quitting is to give employees additional independence and encourage them to use the independence they have. In church, women in leadership can encourage others to think and act independently to stop their quiet quitting from church activities.

Today, I met a church friend at Walmart. She shared that several years ago, she approached the Pastor about starting a Card Ministry. She planned to send a card to congregants, acknowledging significant events in their lives, i.e., the death of a family member, marriage, birthday, graduation, etc. She would sign the card as coming from the church.

When she took the idea to the Senior Pastor, he instructed her on how to do the Card Ministry rather than listening to her ideas. Then, the Senior Pastor took her to the Associate Pastor. The Associate Pastor gave the woman additional advice. Given these overwhelming directions, the woman decided to forgo her planned Card Ministry. She quietly dropped the valuable idea. Currently, a Card Ministry remains a gap in the church. I wonder what would have happened if pastors had encouraged the woman rather than instructed her?

Churches can intentionally borrow from business techniques to promote women's engagement in the church. Ten ways churches can stop women's learned helplessness and quiet quitting behaviors at church are:[9]

1. Schedule regular "brainstorming" sessions, for example, once per month, on a specific topic. Topics could include subjects for educational classes, fun events for children, and mission activities. Remember to encourage women to attend these sessions. Offer free childcare. Get congregants comfortable having input into church programs and strategies. Accept the fact that these sessions may be poorly attended initially until congregants become familiar with the opportunity they offer.

2. Welcome ideas even if those ideas seem far-fetched. Women are creative thinkers and are good at thinking outside the box.

3. Don't respond with defensiveness or dismissiveness. Those responses shut down a woman's input.

4. Never identify how the idea was tried in the past and didn't work. Church congregants change. Past failures don't mean an idea won't be successful today.

5. Get women's input on the best time to offer classes and other events. Women coordinate getting children dressed and out the door. Too early events or late evening events won't work for mothers with children.

6. Don't stick with how the church is currently doing an activity. Shake church activities up.

7. Remember, if congregants aren't aware you are offering an activity, you might as well not be.

8. Be sure to give participants choices. The brain craves choices. The expectation of choice is associated with anticipation and excitement.

9. Add diverse women to committees and activities. Don't always select the same women.

10. Never, never have only one woman on a committee with a bunch of men. Women's ideas will be buried under the weight of men's ideas.

Woman, never be relegated to the committee secretary role.

A woman shared that she was going to quit participating in church dinners. The church has several of these each month to encourage fellowship and a sense of family. She's contributed entrees to meals and is thanked for them, but wants to do more than cook for church events. She wants to use her Bible knowledge and organizational skills in other ways in the church.

This woman is one whom women in church leadership roles want to tap. Her past work and present words and character show that she is ready to move into a more complex church role. Her readiness could be lost if women do not know where the woman is in her willingness to contribute.

Women can hold discussions with other church women to learn their knowledge and skills, and how they want to contribute them to the church. Woman, if you take this type of coordinating role, you are showing Christian character. Then, you can initiate a plan to use the cadre of willing workers. Involvement will keep a woman in the church. In contrast, disregard for her strengths will be the church's loss.

Attraction Power

Research showed that attractive women have more power in a church than unattractive ones; however, attractive power isn't viewed the same by all individuals. Below are four perspectives on church power and attraction.[1,2]

First, in churches, individuals find a woman more attractive if she is like them. They associate with her

more often than with a woman who is different from them, whether that difference is color, accent, etc. Think about individuals in your church. Do you hang out with individuals unlike you? If someone is unlike you, do you ignore them and/or discount what they say? I attended a church women's luncheon. Same income level women talked to each other. They seemed to be a "closed" group; they ignored other women at the table. That action was unkind and not a good advertisement for the event.

Two, attraction encompasses being beautiful; however, beauty is defined by the culture. In an art course, I saw sculptures and paintings of women from the Middle Ages and ancient civilizations. These women were large, but not muscular. In the 21st century, individuals would have ignored or disdained women in these sculptures and paintings. The women in them wouldn't have been memorialized in paintings and sculptures. At this time in the U.S., the ideal woman is tall and slender. In 10 years, the ideal shape of a female model may be different; definitions of beauty and attractiveness change. In churches, women can make a concerted effort to include other women who don't look like the ideal model of 21st-century womanhood.

Society defines what is attractive

Three, often attraction power is based on being "authentic," which in the 21st century means "being real." These women are described as "having a great personality." A great personality can be more important than physical beauty. I watch Dagan McDowell's evening television newscast. By many indicators, Dagan isn't beautiful. Other TV stations have more physically attractive broadcasters. I watch Dagan because she offers "real" opinions.

Fourth, a woman is only attractive in a church if she adapts and respects local customs and protocols. Until the late 20th century, women in my home church were expected to wear dresses or skirts rather than slacks/pants. God forbid if she wore jeans! A woman who wore slacks was avoided and rebuffed regardless of her physical appearance.

Attractive women comply with church norms. Church protocols (church rules, practices, proprieties) often aren't written, but they are set in stone. In my church, when Communion (Eucharist) is offered, grape juice is used. If a woman attempted to introduce wine, her effort would be rejected regardless of her attractiveness. Why? Because the church norm rejects the use of alcohol.

Once identified as attractive, a churchwoman often has a "halo effect." Highly attractive women are rated as more effective speakers and more trustworthy, supportive, and encouraging than moderately attractive ones. Attractive women are identified as friendly, social, and better listeners than unattractive ones. In reality, a woman may have none of these characteristics.

Charisma is an extraordinary amount of attraction power. Charisma draws others like a magnet. Charismatic women are viewed as positive, self-confident, energetic, and eloquent. Often, they are assertive, charming, and present themselves well. Charismatic women appear accessible to others. Sometimes they are accessible; sometimes they aren't. A woman's charisma can be used for good or ill in her church.

A familiar Bible woman who had charisma or, at a minimum, attraction power was Delilah, a Philistine woman. As you read her story, you see that she used

attraction for ill. A Bible Judge, Samson, loved a Philistine woman, Delilah (Judges 16:4-22). Not once did the Bible suggest that Delilah loved Samson, but she entered a relationship with him. When the Philistines learned that Samson spent time with Delilah, they bribed her to learn and reveal to them the secret of Samson's great strength.

When we read the Bible account of Samson and Delilah, they appear to be playing a game. She asked him about the source of his amazing strength. Samson answers with a lie. Delilah relates Samson's lies to the Philistines. The Philistines use the lie to attempt to capture Samson. It didn't work. A rational person would have concluded that Delilah was working with the Philistines. Perhaps Samson's attraction to Delilah wasn't total, but sufficient that Samson didn't put the sequence of events together.

Eventually, Samson told Delilah that the source of his great strength was in his long hair. If his hair were cut, Samson would become as physically weak as other men. While Samson slept, probably in a drunken stupor, Delilah cut Samson's hair. The outcome was Samson's capture by the Philistines.

In the current century, a woman can use attractiveness to get what she wants. At church, attractive women can leverage their appearance to convince others that their perspective is correct. Yet a Christian woman should know that attraction may not have "staying" power. If church women overuse their attraction power, they run the risk of alienating women who aren't as attractive.

Relationship (History) Power

Between women, a relationship develops as they see each other repeatedly, get to know each other, have experiences with each other, and disclose information to each other.[6] In other words, when they have a history with one another. Relationship power is based on trust or, at least, an expectation that a woman will act in a certain way. Trust develops as women see how each other act in various situations, i.e., at a church meal, in Sunday services, and in committee meetings.

Have you ever encountered a woman in church who shows characteristics opposite to the fruit of the Spirit? This churchwoman is impatient, unkind, ungentle, unloving, etc. You may decide that you don't want to be friends with her; you don't trust her. You choose not to be around this woman inside or outside the church. You don't find her attractive. An alternative way to act is to discuss the unkind woman's behavior with her. Possibly, she doesn't know how she presents herself. Maybe she has issues that can be helped by a listening and supportive friend.

As we learn to know a woman, we feel safe around her— or not so safe around her. Encountering another woman weekly at church moves a relationship forward faster than if two women meet only at annual church conferences. A woman's trust in another woman increases with the length and strength of the relationship.

Women from different cultures develop relationships at different speeds. In the U.S., women are willing to form relationships rapidly. In other cultures, i.e., Southeast Asia, women may form them more slowly. It's important that an American woman not conclude that an Asian woman is unwilling to be a friend. Perhaps more time is needed in the relationship.

Enduring human relationships among equals assume reciprocity, that is, both women influence the other. If you assist a churchwoman with a program important to her, you expect that she will assist you with one important to you. If she doesn't, you may withhold your support the next time she needs it. An alternative action is to find out why the churchwoman won't assist you. What is occurring in her life that she couldn't or wouldn't give needed assistance?

Some relationship bonds in church aren't strong, while others are. Relationship power doesn't require admiration; however, it does require acceptance. Relationship power diminishes when something disturbing or repugnant is learned about a woman. A church friend learned that her friend was having a long-term sexual relationship outside of marriage. She stepped back from the friendship. Her exact words were, "I don't feel the same about her." Relationships and relationship power aren't static.

Relationships change over time

Below is a story of two Bible women. Ponder what you can learn from the story that can help your church relationships? Sisters, Leah and Rachel, both married Jacob. These sisters live and work side by side. Rachel was beautiful but barren; Jacob loved Rachel. Jacob didn't love Leah. At the time of this episode, Leah had given birth to four sons to Jacob.

Leah's son (Reuben) brought his mother mandrakes from the field. A cultural belief was that mandrakes promoted fertility. Rachel wanted the mandrakes so she would conceive a son for Jacob. Angrily, Leah replied, "Wasn't it enough that you stole my husband? Now will you steal my son's mandrakes?" (Genesis 30:15). In this story, Leah gave Rachel the mandrakes only when Rachel agreed to give her something.

Rachel and Leah had a complex relationship (history), which included resentment but trust. Leah resented her sister but believed what Rachel told her. Women in a church often have complex relationships.

Final Thoughts

Women with high knowledge power were three times more influential than those with low knowledge power. In the 21st century, many churches are small, with fewer than 100 members. A small church has the advantage that a woman's knowledge and character become clear quickly. In a small church, a major disadvantage is that there are few individuals to do the needed work. Women can't quietly quit or exclude themselves from full participation.

The importance attached to attractiveness varies in different countries and in different eras. Probably, 3000 years ago Israelites rated physical attraction as only moderately important. Other factors, such as familial relationships or wealth, took precedence.

Relationship power doesn't require admiration from other people; however, it does require acceptance.

Attraction and relationship power are highly correlated; so are attraction and character power. Attraction, relationship, and character formed a constellation of power for a woman. At the same time, if a woman has high attraction and relationship powers, but character flaws, her power and influence are diminished greatly.

Points to Ponder

Does your pastor effectively use women's knowledge? How could he/she improve in this area? Are you willing to have a conversation with the pastor about better use of women's knowledge and skills?

List ways to present some, or all, of the ideas from the list of 10 ways to promote women's involvement in your church.

Does a churchwoman's character matter to you? Why and how?

Would your behavior at church be different if you knew you were being watched? How would it change?

Identify a physically beautiful woman whom you consider unattractive. What makes her unattractive?

Of the Bible women identified in this chapter, which ones do you most want to be like? Why?

Chapter 6

Roles and Resources

In Bacon's power model, the second source of power is position[6] Position power encompasses: 1) roles women occupy, 2) resources they control, 3) their reputation, 4) the information a woman has or has access to, and 5) networks they have with others. Deciding whether personal or positional power is more important is hard. The answer depends on the situation and perhaps the values in the church.

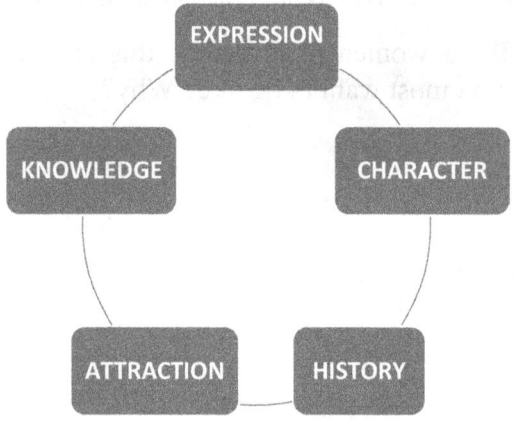

Sources of Position Power

Role Power

Role power is one of the strongest positional power sources.[6] It comes from the positions a woman occupies. In the Bible, those positions included the wife or daughter of an important man; for example, Rizpah was the daughter of Aiah and the concubine of King Saul. In the ancient Near East, a wife's power over family decisions was substantial. No matter how much Jacob wanted out of Paddan Aram, he didn't finalize plans to leave the country until he had agreement from his wives. At the same time, normally, Bible women weren't consulted when fathers/husbands made other types of decisions, such as contracts, purchases.

In the Old Testament, most women were Israelites. In the New Testament, some were Gentiles (non-Israelites). Today, Western Christians aren't identified by nationality. Often, Christian women are identified by the church they attend or their church denomination, i.e., Catholic, Lutheran, or Baptist. Demonstrating the transition to women's individuality in the 21st century, a churchwoman today is described as being in the choir, chairing the Buildings and Grounds Committee, teaching a Sunday school class, or in charge of the nursery rather than by her husband's or father's position.

In the Bible, a daughter accepted that her mother could direct her activities in the home, i.e., to grind grain. A servant conformed to her mistress' directions, i.e., to carry water from the town well. Leah and Rachel directed both of their personal servants to have intercourse with Jacob to conceive children. Both of the servants followed their mistress' directions.

In 21st-century churches, women in power don't have the absolute right to direct other women as seen in Bible episodes. Church women learn and use other techniques to get things done. Research studies showed that role power was correlated with a woman's assertiveness, self-confidence, and use of a compelling tone of voice. Ideally, in a church, a woman uses the authority that goes with her role without being heavy-handed.

Credibility and believability are important features of roles in any setting, but particularly in a church. Generally, role power operates in a limited area or sphere but is nonexistent outside that area. Recently, my church started a Seasoned Christian's group. It's composed of individuals over 50 years of age. The purpose was to nurture aging Christians and equip them for God's calling on their lives in their senior years. The group initiator was a 70-plus-aged woman. She had credibility with other ageing congregants because of her age. If the convenor were a young woman, many elders wouldn't have participated. They would shake their heads and ask, "What can she tell me about this stage of my life?"

In today's church, a woman may have acknowledged expertise as an organ/piano player and choir director, but the woman has no expertise as a Bible teacher. Where do you fit in your church with your skill set? Think about a needed ministry in your church, a gap. Are you at the optimal age to start it? Do you have the needed skills?

Often, power is limited to a specific role or expertise.

Old Testament women with role power were Puah and Shiphrah. They were Israelite midwives in Egypt. If either midwife instructed an Israelite woman to take an action to prevent a miscarriage or manage her pregnancy, the Israelite woman followed the recommendation. At the same time, if Puah or Shiphrah told an Israelite man how to heal whip lash damage to his back, the man would have discounted the midwife's advice. In the latter instance, the midwife advised outside her area of expertise.

A New Testament woman shows us how to act when removed from a position (role). In this situation, the woman wasn't removed from a church position, but the situation is parallel to a modern-day church. While Lois' husband lived, she had positional power in her home. She managed her husband's household, including household resources. Lois' daughter, Eunice, married a non-Jewish man.

When Lois' husband died, Lois went to live with her daughter, Eunice. Lois had no role or power in the Greek household. Lois lost her position as wife and household manager. She no longer had control of household resources, nor could she direct servants' activities. According to the Bible, Lois did not attempt to usurp her daughter's role as female head of household. Instead, she aided Eunice in educating Timothy, Eunice's son and Lois's grandson.

Conceivably, Lois was asked, "How do you feel about losing your position as manager of your deceased husband's household?" We don't know what Lois said as she transitioned into her new role in her daughter's home. From all we read in the Bible, Lois is a model of accepting a secondary role with grace.

Twenty-first-century women aren't socialized into helping (secondary) roles even at church. Nonetheless, the role is a crucial one. Every woman can't be a leader in the church in all situations. Women have a role to support individuals in charge.

Have you ever been in a similar situation at church? For example, you directed the Children's Ministry, then another person was assigned or hired into the role. Naturally, other women ask you about the responsibility change. What answer did you give? How did you exhibit acceptance and support for the new leader versus negativity and petulance? What would Lois do? What would Jesus do?

Where a woman can use role power is limited. A pastor's wife worked in the local school system. In church, when the pastor's wife asked a congregant to do something, generally the congregant did it. In the school system, the pastor's wife didn't have the authority of her husband's position.

In the 21st century, role power depends on consent from individuals who receive direction. Role power of the type, "Do it because I say so," may get compliance but little commitment from colleagues. Always be prepared to give reasons for any direction you give. Often, the first time a woman acts heavy-handed at church, subordinates don't challenge her. They let her behavior slide, even though they may not like it. If she consistently abuses her role power, congregants become agitated, resistance mounts, and a woman's role power decreases.

Abusive Behavior

Throughout history, women have abused other women. Think back to how Sarah, the wife of the wealthy Abraham, treated her servant, Hagar. Sarah couldn't get pregnant, so she directed Abraham to have intercourse with Hagar. This ancient Middle East custom was a common way for infertile wives to claim children. After Hagar became pregnant, Hagar treated Sarah with contempt. Sarah complained to Abraham, who directed Sarah to deal with Hagar's behavior however Sarah desired. The Bible recorded that Sarah treated Hagar so harshly that Hagar ran away. Sarah wasn't held accountable for her abuse of Hagar.

Women's abuse (including bullying) of other women is alive in Christian churches today. Church abuse doesn't mean one woman physically harms another, which likely occurred in Sarah's harsh treatment of Hagar. In 21st-century churches, injury or harm is mental or emotional. As with Sarah, the abuse is most often from a woman in a higher position to a woman in a lower position.

Women abuse others in churches

Much has been written about women abusing other women in the workplace. Not surprisingly, women's abuse in the church looks similar. Some ways a woman in a higher position—with more power—in the church abuses a woman with less power include:

- A woman leader of a Bible study ignores a woman participant who wants to comment.

- A woman Chairperson of a church committee disregards the ideas of a woman on the committee.

- A woman doesn't only disagree with another woman's comments; she openly disparages them and their maker.

- A woman removes another from a position or role. This demoting occurs when a church woman tells another that she's no longer needed in a certain role, i.e., teaching a children's Sunday school class.

- Abuse occurs when one woman shows favoritism to another. Women not favored are ignored, disregarded, and neglected.

As Christian women, we don't have to wonder how to deal with a woman who is an abuser in church. The Bible gives specific instructions on how a woman should deal with a woman who abuses her:

> If your brother or sister sins, go and point out their fault, just between the two of you. But if they will not listen, take one or two others along, so that 'every matter may be established by the testimony of two or three witnesses (Matthew 18:15-17).

The question is, do we make a woman abuser known to the pastor? That is a tough call. If abuse is harming the health of a congregation or the reputation of the church, the answer is "Yes."

Before you have the conversation with your pastor, pray that God's will, not yours, will be done. Determine to be humble and remember you are in this conversation for the long haul.

Organize your thoughts and points you want to make. You may even want to keep a written record of where you believe the abuse occurred. Naming specific situations (even dates) adds strength to your assertion.

The discussion may require more than one meeting. Keep making your point. You believe it's accurate. Don't get sidetracked from your main intent.

Remember, you've been experiencing and praying about the situation for weeks, even months. In contrast, this meeting may be the first time the pastor hears about it. The pastor's first reaction will likely be denial. Just as you needed time to ponder and pray about the situation, so will the pastor. Perhaps you will need to schedule a follow-up meeting.

Don't gossip or otherwise share your pending conversation. True, the Bible instructs us to share our burdens with fellow Jesus-believers. You can solicit needed situational prayers without giving specifics. Saying something as innocuous as, "I am going to have a tense meeting with the pastor and need your prayers," is saying too much. This statement can generate gossip in the church. It's okay and biblical to solicit prayers; however, ask fellow-believers to pray for an unnamed prayer request.

Resource Power

and.[6] A woman has resources through her roles, i.e., title, wife of a man with a substantial position or plenty of money. Generally, a Bible woman in a high role controls more resources than a woman in a lower role.

For Bible women, resources included food supplies and the ability to allocate work; however, there were exceptions. A few Old Testament women owned land, i.e., Zelophehad's daughters. In the New Testament, some women had resources (Joanna, Suzanna, and Mary Magdalene) which they used to support Jesus' itinerant ministry. A New Testament woman, Lydia, owned a business selling purple dye.

Most 21st-century Christian women want to support their church. Few churches can survive without women sharing their resources, including abilities. In a local church, women use their resources, knowing they serve God when serving others. One-upmanship or pride shouldn't be a motive for service.

Women are a church resource

Resource power is only important if someone wants the resources a woman has. For example, does a woman have the money needed for Vacation Bible School (VBS) lunches? Does a woman have time during the day to help with a VBS program? A woman who doesn't work outside the home typically has more hours each week to give to church activities than a woman who has a job. Yet, most women have some discretionary time.

One local church has a group of individuals, mostly women, named Deaconesses. Deaconesses make home and hospital visits and organize food for families who need meals, etc. Deaconesses are elected to the role. The church provides financial support to the Deaconess Ministry. Women give the amount of time they have available. No set number of hours is required. Deaconess leaders understand that women have differing amounts of time to do the ministry work. You may want to start a Deaconess Ministry in your church.

All churches have needs for children's programs and adult education curricula. Most church denominations, as well as independent Christian organizations, have online curricula that can be accessed to aid a woman's teaching efforts. A woman with more discretionary time can develop her own curriculum. One semester, I volunteered to teach middle school children one Sunday a month. The curriculum was set. That was about five years ago; I still remember what a good time I had.

Think about your church. What is needed? Meet with other church women, maybe even some men. Do you all see common needs? Several weeks ago, several women in my church identified that we don't have a church Benevolence Committee. All benevolence requests go to the pastor, who decides when and how the church should honor requests. That structure is part of the pastor's workload. By initiating a Benevolence Committee with written guidelines for allocating resources, women became more involved in the church operations, and the pastor has one less job to do.

Ideally, the church has an organized plan to access church women's resources. Many women want to share their resources but need direction on how to do it.

Research on resource power found that resource-rich women don't always thrive in a church.[10] Their failure may be their own doing. At times, they appear insensitive to others' feelings and needs. They may have little insight into what others value and therefore have difficulty building close relationships. Others in the church don't want to work with them. Often, these women are unable to resolve conflicts and disagreements because they expect to have their way. Women with strong interpersonal skills can facilitate resource-rich women's desire to share.

Hoarding resources and/or using resources as a means of coercing others is a power strategy, but a strategy that isn't consistent with God's direction for using resource power:

> Do not withhold good from those who deserve it when it is in your power to help them (Proverbs 3:27).

Below are two stories on resources controlled by women. One woman lived in the Old Testament and one in the New Testament.

Abigail's husband was a wealthy farmer in ancient Israel. Nabal pastured flocks near Mount Carmel, where David and his men hid from King Saul. David's men protected Nabal's flocks and herders. When Nabal was shearing his sheep, David sent men to Nabal and asked for food. David expected that Nabal would share his resources with the men who protected his flocks.

Shockingly, Nabal refused, even insulting David's men. Nabal didn't see the need or didn't know how to build mutually beneficial relationships.

When David heard about Nabal's actions, he determined to kill every male in Nabal's household.

Servants told Abigail about Nabal's treatment of David's men. She was appalled! Immediately, Abigail gathered food, put it on donkeys, and went to meet David and his men. Abigail pleaded with David not to kill members of Nabal's homestead. David accepted the supplies and turned aside his anger from Nabal's household.

Nabal's behavior exemplified some of the negative research findings about control of resources. Abigail was an exception to research findings. She was attractive and knew how to manage abundant resources. Do you want to be like Nabal or Abigail?

Lydia was a Jewish businesswoman who operated in Philippi. One Sabbath, Lydia and a group of women met to pray on a riverbank outside of Philippi. Paul joined them and shared the good news of Jesus, the Christ. Lydia converted to Christianity and was baptized. Then, Lydia opened her home to Paul and fellow evangelists to stay in. She provided them with a place to sleep and food. Lydia shared her resources with Paul and colleagues for most of the three months they remained in Philippi.

Final Thoughts

Having high role power versus low role power doubles a woman's ability to achieve goals; yet Bacon's theory of power found that high role power isn't as important as personal (expressiveness, knowledge, relationship, attraction, or character) powers.

Examining Bible history and culture caused me to conclude that role power could have been more important in the Bible era than it is in the 21st century, but their role power was in a limited area, i.e., wife and mother. Never in recorded history have women had such extensive role power as they do in the 21st century.

Resource power is the weakest of all power sources, highly correlated with role power. In a church, a woman with a high role generally controls more resources. For example, the head of the Choir frequently chooses hymns that will be sung. She decides who will have solo pieces.

Points to Ponder

What happens in a church when a woman's resources are substantially reduced, for example, if she is divorced from her high-status husband or if her business fails? Is she then discounted by other churchwomen? Could she conclude that the church only wanted her resources, not herself?

How should you behave in your church when you are aware that you have more resources than most other individuals in the church? Be as specific as possible.

Have you ever been moved into a lesser role in your church? What happened? How did you feel?

Have you ever seen a woman, or even children, abused in church? What did you do? If you did nothing, do you remain content with your action?

Chapter 7

Known and Knowing

In addition to Role and Resource, Bacon[6] proposed three other types of Positional Power: reputation, information, and network. These power sources provide insight into a biblical woman's success and how 21st-century women can operate successfully in their church. As a woman who has been in churches for 40 years, I resonate with these three sources of positional power more than with role and resource power.

Reputation Power

Reputation is one of the most important power sources a woman has. A woman's reputation is what others think of her.[6] A good reputation makes a woman appear better and more skilled in every way.

> *Reputation is a rising tide that lifts all boats* [6]

According to the Bible, the operation manual for ancient Israelites and Christians, "A good reputation is better than costly perfume" (Ecclesiastes 7:1). In Bible times, a woman's reputation was based on her actions. Her good deeds were more valuable than any material possession, outward appearances, or the most luxurious perfume. Often, character power (a personal power source) and reputation (a positional power source) went together.

A superficial look at 21st-century society suggests that reputation is based on skills, i.e., professional sports ability, musical talents. A deeper dive shows that if inappropriate words or actions become known, skills and positions aren't enough to save a woman's reputation.

Bible women and 21st-century women with good (high) reputations build rapport and trust with other women and with men. Reputation is relayed through individuals who praise or criticize. In Proverbs, the ideal wife was praised by her husband's colleagues. Collegial praise enhanced the woman's reputation and her husband's status in a community.

In a church, a woman's reputation is predicated on adhering to social norms.[1,10] At the same time, universal character strengths exist that enhance a woman's reputation. Courage and the ability to overcome fear are valued in every culture, including church culture.

It takes time to build a good reputation. A Bible woman lived in the same place most of her life; neighbors knew her character. Often, the woman's reputation accompanied her in the community.

In the 21st-century church, a woman doesn't come to her church with a positive reputation. Although some congregants may know her, most don't. She needs to get to know congregants and often work in sundry roles to evolve a reputation. A woman's church reputation is a group consensus, a shared opinion, of her value, merit, or ability that only develops over time.

Below are seven strategies for a churchwoman to think about as she builds her church reputation.[10]

1. Is authentic – doesn't have a church face and another face for other places.

2. Has a strong work ethic – meets deadlines, goes the extra mile.

3. Talks positively to and about others. Positivity includes being polite and tactful and giving credit to others. No one builds a good reputation by complaining.

4. Has integrity, is honest, and does what is right.

5. Is a good communicator – Familiarizes yourself with how others communicate (email, text message) so you can reach them. When I started attending my current church, I didn't use text messages; however, text messages were normative in the church. I had to transition from email to texts.

6. Manages her online presence. Fellow church members should never be shocked by pictures and words on social media accounts.

7. Dresses appropriately for church. High heels and fur coats are out of place for my present church but were common in a previous church. What about your church? Try to dress at the normative level of your church.

A person at the center of a large network of individuals can disproportionately influence a woman's reputation. If a powerful church individual, i.e., pastor, says good things about a woman, her power increases. At the same time, powerful individuals can reduce a woman's reputation power. I've seen a mere lift of an eyebrow or grimace from a pastor/church leader cause a woman's church reputation to plummet.

In the Bible, an extraordinary reputation wasn't always the same as a good reputation. An Old Testament woman had an excellent reputation for doing what she said she could do; however, no one called her good.

A Canaanite woman who lived in the town of Endor. King Saul wanted to consult with the dead prophet Samuel about a pending battle with the Philistines. He wanted someone who could bring up Samuel's spirit. His men found the Canaanite woman, known as the Witch of Endor. She could speak with spirits.

A disguised King Saul went to the Witch of Endor's home. The witch brought up Samuel's spirit. Samuel told King Saul that the Israelites would lose the upcoming battle with the Philistines; he and his sons would be killed. Can you imagine the magnitude of the Witch of Endor's reputation after this event came true? Not only did she call up dead Samuel's spirit, but every word spoken by Samuel came true.

Information Power

As a woman in a church, there is information that you 1) need to know, 2) want to know, and 3) have no interest in knowing. Getting, interpreting, and reporting data are keys to information power.[6] I'm not writing about gossip, i.e., whose daughter made Dean's list, who wore a too-tight dress, or who is dating whom. I'm writing about solid information that makes you a success in a church position.

Not only must a woman access information in her church, but she must put that information into the context of what else is happening in the church; she must interpret her data (information). Then she must report the information, along with what it means to her pastor or the leadership structure. Only after having done all three (acquire, interpret, and report) does a woman have the potential for information power.

In each of her roles (head of the Benevolence Committee, children's Sunday School teacher, member of the Leadership Team, etc.), a woman acquires power if she accesses, interprets, and reports information correctly. When she doesn't access and use information correctly, she loses information credibility.

Before starting to collect information (data, evidence, etc.), a woman should ask, "What do I want to know?" For example, I want to know how many programs the church has for middle-aged adults and seniors. Possibly, she may add, "How well are the programs attended?" "Are our current programs meeting the needs of our middle and older adult members?" Carefully contemplate your motive for accessing the information. Hopefully, it's never to show another church person how wrong they are or to get praise. Yes, selfish reasons for getting information can even occur in church!

In the getting information stage of information power, information includes evidence, facts, statistics, knowledge, and news. Most Bible women got information from family, neighbors, visitors, and merchants. God talked to some women directly, i.e., the prophetesses Deborah and Huldah, and to Manoah's wife. In the 21st century, one way God talks to women is through the Bible. A woman won't get a message from God that contradicts Holy Scripture.

At times, the information Bible women and men wanted was the same, but they used it differently. For example, both Bible women and men wanted information on crop yields. A man wanted the information to decide which crops to plant in his fields and how to sell his crops. A woman's concern was feeding her household. At other times, Bible women and men wanted different information. A man wanted to know how to make iron farm implements or weapons. A woman wanted information on the availability of fabric yarn that could be made into clothes.

In 21st-century churches, the same patterns occur. At times, men and women want the same information, i.e., the budget. At other times, churchmen and women want different information. An example could be that men are more interested in who oversees the church building and grounds, while women may be more interested in education programs.

One way of getting background data on a topic is to do an internet search. If you do an internet search, many articles appear. You can even watch videos on a topic. Be sure to confirm that the writer or producer has values consistent with those of your church.

Confirm the posted date of the articles. For example, if you are tasked with making a recommendation for a new sound system, be sure to choose recently posted articles. Some internet search articles are outdated. Postings on the internet are rarely removed; a search may reveal articles posted 10 years earlier. You could recommend a sound system several generations outdated unless you read up-to-date articles.

Recently, I attempted to edit the church website. I searched for technical articles on how to make changes. I had to make sure articles were written and posted after the last web host updates were made. If I didn't note the article's postdate, I could attempt to make changes to the website based on outdated material. My changes and I could waste a lot of time.

Where can women get information about what is happening in their church?

- Church website

- Minutes of church council (vestry) and committee meetings. Often these minutes are found on a common bulletin board.

- Newsletters, Sunday bulletins.

- Church social media sites, e.g., Facebook, X.

- Sunday verbal announcements.

- Informal conversations among congregants.

Church information is more than Sunday morning announcements.

Interpreting information: Women must make sense of the information they collect; that's named interpretation, how pieces of data, evidence, etc. fit together. Interpretation is a crucial step when building information power.

Before starting to interpret information (data, evidence, etc.), a woman again asks, "What do I want to know? What problem needs a solution? What does this information mean to me in my local church?" At this point, she will likely include some and discard other pieces of information. Naturally, some initially collected data won't be relevant. You can refile or discard it.

The woman must ask if she needs more information. If so, what is needed? A woman can't interpret data correctly if she is missing a crucial piece of information. She could come to the wrong conclusion. Can you imagine reporting information to your church and being told, "Yes, but you didn't include preschoolers in your data on children attending the Children's program."

Nothing ruins a woman's credibility in church more than that type of statement when a woman gives a presentation. That's why gathering all relevant information is mandatory.

Getting more information can be draining. At times, a woman is tempted to conclude she has done enough work on this project and stop before all evidence is collected. Remember, all information isn't equal. Accurate, relevant, and scarce information is most valuable. Accurately interpreting scarce information increases a woman's information power.

Recently, I learned that a newly widowed churchwoman with several children was having significant financial difficulties. When I met with the senior pastor about the woman's hardship, he told me that the church had assisted her with a substantial amount of money recently. I was in a quandy. When is giving money "enough"? Are there other ways I could help this woman? You can ask yourself the same questions.

Mine is a small community church. We have fewer than 100 members. Over 50% are women; at least five are single mothers. Our organizational chart is flat with 1-2 committees, including the church Leadership

Committee. Mostly, we operate as a large family. But perhaps we need more committees to maximize efficiency, reduce the workload of the pastor, and ensure all the needed church work gets done. What about your church? Can you identify any needed committees?

Are certain committees needed in every church?

Reporting Information: Bible and 21st-century women had power when they shared information with the right people at the right time. In most churches, reporting information focuses on telling stories about a situation rather than reporting statistics. Most congregants aren't going to appreciate an analysis of variance significance level. Regardless of how information is reported, the report must be accurate and easily understood. When a woman tells a story, she crafts it so that the focus remains anonymous. That's not always easy in a small church.

Depending on presentation styles acceptable in her church, a woman can use a podium and screen presentation or a more casual style, i.e., chairs in a circle or at a table. Style doesn't matter as much as accuracy and comfort. Generally, handouts are a good idea.

In the New Testament, a wife (Priscilla) and husband (Aquila) had information power. Priscilla and Aquila heard a visitor, Apollos, speaking in the Ephesus synagogue. Apollos was a learned Jewish scholar who spoke eloquently about the coming of the Messiah, but Apollos knew only the baptism of repentance preached by John the Baptist. Apollo didn't know that Jesus had come to Earth.

After the synagogue meeting, Priscilla and Aquila invited Apollos to their home, probably for a meal. They shared information on the life and death of Jesus and that Jesus was the expected Jewish Messiah. Notably, the couple waited until after the meeting to share their information. They didn't embarrass Apollo by contradicting his teaching in the synagogue.

By Priscilla and Aquila sharing their information about Jesus at an optimal time and place, a strong missionary voice was added to the new Christian church. Think about how you could apply Priscilla and Aquilla's example of sharing information in your church.

Network Power

Network power is about who you know and/or who is a part of your circle.[6] Networks are connections between women and others who live, work, and socialize together. Those connections can occur daily, weekly, monthly, or over an even longer period, for example, at community church conferences.

Networks can be on social media. I have friends on social media that I have never met in person. They have power over me, and I have power over them, possibly because we've communicated over the years.

Bible women communicated ideas and expertise (how to do tasks) to network connections. Before the advent of written and electronic communications, some women were "connectors." They seemed to know everyone and everything that was happening in their environments. How does being a connector differ from being a gossip?

I volunteer at a women's center once a week. One woman employee keeps me up to date on what's going on in the organization, i.e., "management decided to……" She is careful not to give personal opinions about decisions; she gives information. She is a network connector.

Connectors occur in every church. In 21st-century Western churches, network power doesn't exist on its own. Rather, network power merges from other power sources, i.e., role, resources, information, knowledge, and attraction. Network power can be transitory. It can be lost if a woman 1) refuses to reciprocate once a favor is done for her; 2) moves out of a position or role, or 3) does something so repugnant that individuals no longer want to associate with her.

Most church networks and the power in them are of three types:[6]

1. Strong versus weak networks

2. Formal versus informal networks

3. Dense versus thin networks

A woman who aspires to have power in her church should evaluate the church's networks. As I outline each of these three types of networks, women may conclude that the information isn't relevant: it's even boring. It is neither! If you want power in your church, think about each of these networks. Who do you need to get to know if you want church power?

<u>Strong/Weak Networks</u>: Bible women's strongest networks were individuals they knew best and/or communicated with most. Often, strong networks are family ties and/or a mutual interest in staying in touch. As a girl, my aunts, uncles, and cousins attended the same church as my immediate family. We were a strong network in the church.

Now, my family is five hours away; however, I have two women friends, whom I met at church. We are about the same age and have many of the same spiritual interests. We get together outside of church for lunches and coffee. The three of us are a strong network. Women should treasure their strong networks. These are the women who help us get things done in the church. They keep you connected with others in the church. They give you information.

In my former church, a group of women has been in a Tuesday morning Bible study for about 25 years. The 12 or so of them were a strong network. The primary way they connected was by sharing prayer requests. That's how they found out what was occurring in each other's lives.

A challenge in trying to enter this strong network was that they knew life events about each other that occurred over time. I didn't know them. I had little history with individual group members and/or their families. When they shared their prayer requests, I couldn't relate to all the names provided. Church women's groups must work out ways to enfold newcomers.

Although strong network relationships are important to women, so are weak ones. A Bible woman saw some women irregularly, perhaps only at the synagogue occasionally.

Weak network connections are valuable in 21st-century churches. They provide women with information and resources beyond those available in their strong church network. Another example of a woman's weak network is a woman she talks with at an annual religious festival in Jerusalem. A woman can get information from such a casual network colleague. At a minimum, she can learn concerns and opinions of women in other parts of the country.

In the 21st century, a churchwoman doesn't know well all the women in her church. These women are part of the woman's weak network. The woman said "Hi, how are you?" when they see each other, but don't engage in an in-depth conversation. Yet these women are important. Because they know you, they may vote for you for a church office or possibly assist you with a needed church project. Weak network connections are valuable in 21st-century churches. They provide women with information and resources beyond those available in their strong church network.

Formal/Informal Networks: Many women's networks are formal. Last evening, a church women's group met. We are a formal church group; we are listed as a church organization. There is a leader appointed by the pastor. Membership is all women in the church. We meet once a month for supper and catch up on each other's lives. The group's purpose is fellowship. Bible study isn't included. This group is fluid; the number of attendees varies. Some meetings have as few as three women attending. At others, there are 12 of us. This formal network has a name and even a social media page.

My church has another group that I am part of. It is an informal group. For example, 6-9 of us get together for dinner once a month. We discuss spiritual issues, such as when it is okay to tell a lie. We meet outside the church at a restaurant or more often in a member's home for a potluck supper. Some churches would name this a Life Group, but we don't have that structure in our church. This group is my local family.

Dense/Thin Networks: Dense information networks occur when several women have many links among themselves. There's a high level of interconnectedness. In dense networks, information flows fast because of multiple interconnections. The downside of a dense network is redundancy. A woman may hear the same information from several sources. If you want to impact your church, you have a better chance of success if you are part of a dense network.

A thin network has fewer connections. In them, women are connected to only a few others. Information flows more slowly with little repetition. Not all women in church know each other and prefer it that way. A church includes different types of individuals. Some are introverted; others are extroverted. Assume different women want different types of fellowship, or even no fellowship, from the church. Don't try to put all women into the same network.

Final Thoughts

Women with better reputations have more power than those with a poorer reputation. Two personal power sources, knowledge and expressiveness, are correlated with a woman's reputation.

The importance of information can't be overestimated. Accurate information to make a major church decision has three steps: acquiring, interpreting, and reporting information.

Ideally, you get information from a variety of information sources, but your primary source is God. God is your number one network connector. No, I don't mean by way of the pastor's sermons. I'm referring to reading the Bible and praying.

What are your major information sources?

Today, network power is present in every culture. Of the many countries where network power was studied, Israel ranked the highest in valuing, having, and using networks.

Having a large social network can triple a woman's power to influence others. Not all network relationships turn into friendships. Some network relationships remain weak; they are still valuable.

Points to Ponder

Why would the writer of Ecclesiastes conclude that "A good reputation is more valuable than costly perfume" (Ecclesiastes 7:1)? Do you agree or disagree?

If you were giving a churchwoman advice on how to repair her reputation, what advice would you include?

Huldah's major source of information was God. How can your major source of information be God?

Who are the women with information power in your church? If you were to rate each of these women on each fruit of the Spirit, what would be your conclusions?

In some churches, the Leadership Committee meeting minutes were posted on a bulletin board. What are the pros and cons of disseminating information this way? What are alternative ways to disseminate this type of information?

If a 21st-century woman wants network power in her church, what should she do? How can you cultivate a network of women?

An old adage says that success depends less on what you know and more on whom you know. Why do you believe nor not believe that this statement is true.

Chapter 8

Willpower in You

Some churchwomen have tremendous willpower.[6] Generally, willpower isn't associated with heredity. Instead, willpower is related to the environment where a woman is reared and/or finds herself.

No one gives a woman willpower—not her parents, pastors, or teachers.[6] Willpower originates in a woman and is unique to her, but manifests differently in different women. Willpower can overcome a myriad of disadvantages, such as being born in poverty or a racial minority.

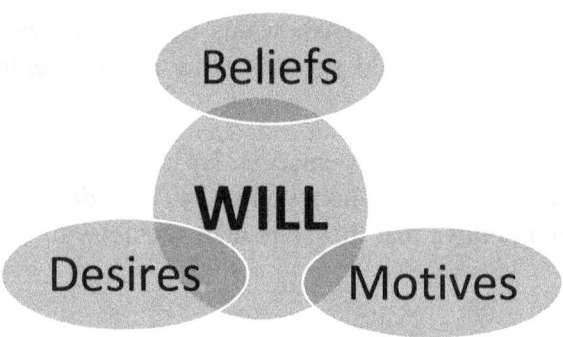

Sources of Willpower

Willpower helps women to grow spiritually. It's a gift from God. It begins with a determination to make something happen, yet willpower is more than a determination or desire. Willpower involves action.

Church women with willpower dare to act and to persist in the face of opposition, even failure. This woman is unwilling to be defeated.

Biblical women demonstrated willpower when they acted to change a situation, i.e., Pharaoh's daughter acted to save Moses from the Nile River. Imagine the Israelite nation without Moses. A Bible woman's willpower is separate from her nationality. Some Bible women with willpower were Israelites and Egyptians. Ruth was a Moabite, and Rahab was a Canaanite.

The question that every woman who takes her faith seriously and expresses it in her church is, "Do I have willpower?"

Viewpoints on Willpower

Management guru Terry Bacon called willpower a "mega-source of power," claiming it magnified every other power source.[6] According to Walt Whitman,[11] character and willpower were the only investments worth making.

Nothing great was achieved without willpower!

McNair[12] wrote, "No will means no capacity for making moral choices." No will means no responsibility for sin. Faults and shortcomings are blamed on genetics, background, parents, environment, or just "bad luck."

In the Bible, willpower is named "self-control." Self-control is from God, i.e., God gave us a spirit not of fear, but of power, love, and self-control. God said that self-control is crucial for success in life. Gaining control of the will is crucial to inner peace. Ultimately, self-control allows women to use their energies to advance God's plan both for themselves and their church. The self-control identified in the Bible, particularly in the letters to first-century churches, is different from the willpower that Bacon uses in his model.[6]

A Bible woman's willpower came not from an impulse to act, but from acting (judiciously) on a desire, motive, or belief. The same principle applies to 21st-century women. For Bible women and 21st-century women, willpower is a significant asset where non-Christians and/or men dominate much of society, culture, and church decision-making activities.

At times, women run into gender differences in willpower in churches—often, men express more willpower than women in church settings. Women, don't be surprised to see gender differences in your church.

Because men demonstrate more willpower than women is no reason for women to deny their willpower. Often, a woman with strong willpower needed nothing but her own actions to change her environment. Think of the prophets Miriam, Deborah, and Hannah. At times, a woman's actions changed the situation for the better, as in the case of Tamar (Judah's daughter-in-law) and Jael. Women with strong wills influenced Bible history and influence churches today.

Components of Willpower

Willpower encompasses beliefs, desires, and motives, all of which lead to actions. Belief is a sure feeling that something is true or exists. Beliefs are convictions. In church, a woman's beliefs about God, spirituality, and religion are named "faith."

Our beliefs could be wrong!!!!

In contrast to beliefs, which come from mental processes, desires come from emotions.[6] A desire is a conscious impulse or want that usually brings enjoyment or satisfaction. Examples of women's desires include pastoring a church and birthing a child. These desires can be intense and all-consuming.

Motives are enticements, incentives, or impulses. Generally, motives are tied more closely to emotions than to beliefs. Women have both positive and negative emotions. Sometimes, negative emotions are stronger than positive ones and may result in stronger desires. Don't you think more often about what you did wrong than what you did right? Your thoughts are related to negative emotions more than positive emotions.

A churchwoman's motives can be internal or external. An internal motivator—intrinsic motivator—comes from inside a woman. An example is a church woman who assists with vacation Bible school because she believes children need to learn about Jesus and the Bible. Further, the woman finds satisfaction working with children.

Performing tasks in the church to look good or please the pastor are external motivators. External motivations are more difficult to sustain than internal ones. The source of an extrinsic motive may disappear if a woman's values change.

Don't Neglect Action

If a component of willpower is action, and if a woman refuses to act, then she had/has no willpower in relation to this pursuit. A cog in the willpower wheel is missing; that is, action is missing. The Bible recorded few, if any, stories of women who refused to act. Their names or stories aren't told in the Bible. Think about Bible stories of women who acted, i.e., Tamar, Jael, Phoebe. All did something; they acted because they believed they should act.

In today's church, God's spirit stimulates a woman to act. An example is the Holy Spirit leading a woman to teach a Sunday school class. What if this woman is frightened of speaking in front of a group? What if she refuses to teach the class? In this scenario, the woman's willpower doesn't overcome her fear. Likely, stories about this churchwoman won't be told. She won't be remembered in the church.

In contrast to women who refuse to act are women who have the willpower to act and do act. A churchwoman shared that she believed God's spirit wanted her to go on a church missionary trip to Central America. The Bible directs Christians to take the Good News of Christ to all people. Her desire is consistent with Jesus' direction to Christian women. Before she initiated fundraising, applied for a passport, purchased an airline ticket—all activities that take willpower on her part—she stopped to pray and requested prayer from her church sisters.

Using Willpower

Willpower is a valuable tool for Christians to use as they live a life pleasing to God. Willpower is a must for Christian women to function successfully in 21st-century churches.

God-given desires are good, acceptable, and perfect. A woman's actions derived from her willpower can be good. Alternatively, some women's willpower-generated actions aren't good. Think about Queen Jezebel and Athaliah's actions while queens. Both women had willpower. Neither used their willpower for good.

When Jesus in Revelation addressed Jezebel (about 1500 years after Queen Jezebel's life) in the Thyatiran church, he said that both Jezebel and her followers would be condemned. In Revelation, Jezebel was named a prophetess and a teacher; yet she led some congregants from true faith in Jesus Christ to idolatry and sexual immorality. She averred that nothing done in the body (i.e., lying, cussing, stealing, sexual immorality) mattered to salvation.

In the 21st century, women can mimic Jezebel's behavior and teach error and depravity. Also, church women must investigate what others are teaching for consistency with the Bible. Are you, woman, reading the Bible daily to know that you and church teachers are staying on track with God's Word?

Christian women want to participate in God's plan for the world. Thus, they try to ensure that their actions are part of God's sovereign will. Often, Western women are so caught up in their own lives that they believe they are correct in all they do.

Satan's temptations can be so subtle that church women aren't aware they are being deceived. I write Christian non-fiction books. At one time, my motive for writing books was to make money and for prestige, rather than to glorify God. My spiritual husband pointed out that my reasons were inconsistent with my avowed desire to serve God. Eventually, I got my head on straight. Now, I write to worship God.

I have strong desires and strong willpower. Often, I conclude that I know what is best for my home and my church. When a situation went wrong because of my actions, I often denied that I did anything wrong. After all, I am a Christian. How could I be wrong when my actions were (ostensibly) for God's glory? Others had to be wrong, but certainly not I. Denial is a strong defense mechanism. Hopefully, women reading this book will never behave as I did.

While willpower is important, it's essential to remember that willpower should be used in conjunction with faith, grace, and reliance on God's power.

Self-Control VS Willpower

Although this chapter and book focus on Bacon's definition of willpower, self-control is part of willpower. When the Bible refers to a woman's will, it mainly means her self-control. Women can use their self-control/willpower for good or ill. Writing to the church at Rome, Paul cautioned that individuals needed to test their desires to discern if they were from God.

Women can use their self-control/willpower to stop criticizing their churches in much the same way they use self-control to stop overeating chocolates. Constantly criticizing your church puts a strain on you and your view of the church. According to Dr. Kelly McGonigal[13] in *The Willpower Instinct,* the urge to criticize is a craving.

McGonigal argued that when a woman has an urge to criticize, she should pause and feel (experience) the urge. Does she feel tense anywhere in her body? For example, does she itch? Where? What happens with her heart rate, to her breathing? Is she irritated? If she says something (criticizes the church), will she get the feelings out of her body? Alternatively, if she uses her self-control and/or willpower to suppress her words, do feelings get worse?

McGonigal[13] contended that when a woman resists a desire using willpower alone, she succeeds only about half the time. 50% is not a high score for an attribute known as "a mega source of power." How can we do better—up that 50% score to at least an 80% score? Fifty percent is failing; 80% is passing. I believe the answer is using Godly self-control.

Discipline and Obedience: In the church, women are outstanding examples of disciplined, obedient Christians. In the Bible, God gave humankind instructions needed for a successful Christian life. What women do with those instructions is up to them. Through their willpower and self-control, women obey God's instruction and live a saved and progressively sanctified—or not—life. God gave women free will to choose. Seeing other women resisting temptation and living a Godly life makes it easier for each of us to do so.

Provide Service: If a church didn't have women, I estimate that 60-70% of the church wouldn't operate with any ease. Women use their willpower to volunteer time and talents for church activities and contribute to the church community. Often, it's women who prepare pastries for snacks before church, contribute food for potluck meals, and visit shut-in church members and members hospitalized.

Participate in Devotions and Bible Study: Women use their willpower to consistently involve themselves in prayer, study scripture, and have personal devotions. Notice I wrote "consistently." Some days, I am like a manual gear-shift car; I can't get my mind and body out of first gear. I don't want to go to Bible study. Some of those other churchwomen annoy me. I've studied that topic previously. I have to use my willpower and my self-control to show up for Bible study and prayer meeting with something approaching a positive attitude.

Ministry: Think about, even list, the ministries in your church, i.e., nursery, children's Sunday school, youth activities, and grounds care. Now, identify the ones that women *aren't* involved in. There are very few of them. A woman's willpower causes her to be active in many church ministries. Because of a woman's willpower, she shows up and contributes.

Lot's daughters had willpower. After Lot and his two daughters escaped Sodom, they went to live in a mountain cave. Eventually, Lot's daughters discussed who would provide for them after their father died.

The daughters developed a plan to secure their future. On successive nights, each daughter got Lot drunk and raped him. Both became pregnant by Lot. Both pregnancies resulted in sons, Moab (father of the Moabites) and Ben-Ammi (father of the Ammonites). The daughters' actions were morally depraved. The best that can be said of the two is that they saw a problem and acted to solve it; they had willpower.

Perhaps as much as 2000 years after the episode with Lot's daughters, a New Testament woman used willpower to get what they wanted. She had a continual flow of vaginal blood for 12 years. She spent all her money going to physicians to get cured. Physicians couldn't stop the bleeding. Because of her vaginal bleeding, she couldn't go to the Temple to worship or have normal social interactions in Jewish society.

The woman heard Jesus was nearby. She thought, "If I just touch his clothes, I will be healed" (Mark 5:28). She braved the crowd and touched Jesus' cloak. Immediately, Jesus felt healing power leave him. He stopped and asked who touched him. When Jesus heard the woman's story, he assured the woman that her faith had healed her. What a beautiful story of a woman's willpower, combined with Jesus' eagerness to heal a daughter.

Final Thoughts

Willpower is more than control of your body. Jesus-focused willpower is your beliefs, desires, and motives. constrained and stimulated by God; they are from God. God gives them to you. God expects women to act on them in churches.

A Bible woman's willpower came not from an impulse to act, but from acting on a desire, motive, or belief. The same principle applies to 21st-century women. Women's willpower is a significant asset in churches; however, only if women are willing to be led by God.

What needs to be done in your church? Don't complain—act. Do something to meet the need. If you see a need, confirm you are seeing accurately with the Pastor or the leadership council. Then, act to solve the problem, be it a Card Ministry, a Senior get-together for fellowship, or greeting congregants as they enter the church.

Modern-day women want to be part of God's plan for Earth rather than only asking God to meet their personal wants. Search the Scriptures to discern requirements for a godly life. Then, pray to be in God's will before acting on a belief, desire, or motive. Although some actions may be allowed by the Bible, not all allowable actions are consistent with God's will for an individual woman's life.

The Bible calls willpower self-control. Absolutely, a Christian woman must have self-control to consistently and constantly show Christ-like behavior. A woman's willpower and self-control work hand in hand to honor God. When I imagine self-control, I think of constraining my worst behaviors through self-control while allowing the fruit of the Spirit to shine in my life.

Points to Ponder

Is willpower an inherent trait of a woman, or is it situational?

Do you have willpower? How do you know? Are you prone to act or remain inactive?

What is the difference between willpower and self-control?

From where do your beliefs and motives come, i.e., cultural norms, societal beliefs, Bible tenets, etc.?

Have you ever had an intense desire to act, but did nothing? How did you exhibit willpower in that situation?

Name some Bible women with a high level of willpower in addition to the ones identified in this chapter. Which ones acted for good and for evil?

How can Satan co-opt a woman's willpower?

Have you ever seen a 21st-century woman who used willpower to achieve, or try to achieve, not-so-good actions? What happened? Describe situations.

Chapter 9

Evaluating Your Power

At this point, you have read about women in the church, how to be an ethical church contributor, and about willpower, a mega source of power in women. Now you get to complete a self-assessment of your power-focused actions in church. Self-assessments are hard because takers benefit optimally only if they answer statements honestly. Originally, Bacon developed this assessment for managers. I adapted it for women in churches.

Directions for completing Power Self-Assessment[6]: How powerful are you, woman, in your church? This self-assessment is designed to help you gauge your sources of personal and positional power as well as your strength of will. Then, helps you to identify areas for improvement. As you respond to statements, be as realistic and honest as possible. For each item, indicate on the scale of 1 to 10 how accurately each statement describes you. Circle 1 if the statement isn't at all true of you and 10 if the statement is very true of you.

Personal Power

Knowledge Power

1. I am highly knowledgeable and skilled in areas of importance to the people I work with in church.
   (No) 1 2 3 4 5 6 7 8 9 10 (Yes)

2. My areas of expertise are special enough that they differentiate me from most other people.
(No) 1 2 3 4 5 6 7 8 9 10 (Yes)

3. Many people are aware of my knowledge and skill in my church and value me for it.
(No) 1 2 3 4 5 6 7 8 9 10 (Yes)

4. I have many symbols of knowledge power, i.e., degrees, titles, awards, publications, certifications.
(No) 1 2 3 4 5 6 7 8 9 10 (Yes)

Knowledge power score summed x 2 = ____

Expressive Power

1. I am a gifted and experienced speaker. I use language well. I speak clearly, concisely, and effectively.
(No) 1 2 3 4 5 6 7 8 9 10 (Yes)

2. In meetings, I participate more than most people and make more comments or suggestions. I usually have more presence in the group than other people.
(No) 1 2 3 4 5 6 7 8 9 10 (Yes)

3. I often communicate to everyone or large groups in my church. I am known as an excellent writer and speaker.
(No) 1 2 3 4 5 6 7 8 9 10 (Yes)

4. I frequently communicate my ideas through writing books, papers, curriculum, blogs; appearing on television or radio programs; using social media; and speaking at conferences.
(No) 1 2 3 4 5 6 7 8 9 10 (Yes)

Expressive power score is sum x 3 = ___

History (Relationship) Power

1. I am very good at building close relationships with other people. I have quite a few church friends and colleagues.
    (No) 1 2 3 4 5 6 7 8 9 10 (Yes)

2. I excel at making connections with people I have just met. Outgoing and friendly, I can establish rapport and trust with others fairly quickly.
    (No) 1 2 3 4 5 6 7 8 9 10 (Yes)

3. I join groups. I am on church committees and teams. I regularly interact with people with common interests.
    (No) 1 2 3 4 5 6 7 8 9 10 (Yes)

4. I am very active on social networking sites, i.e., X, Facebook, LinkedIn, etc.
    (No) 1 2 3 4 5 6 7 8 9 10 (Yes)

History power score is summed x 1 = ___

Attraction Power

1. I have the qualities most people like. I rarely do anything that would offend anyone or cause others to think that I am arrogant, pushy, or distant.
    (No) 1 2 3 4 5 6 7 8 9 10 (Yes)

2. I take care of my appearance, and most people consider me physically attractive or charming.
    (No) 1 2 3 4 5 6 7 8 9 10 (Yes)

3. I am outgoing and very good at engaging people. People enjoy being with me; many of them think I am funny or interesting.
(No) 1 2 3 4 5 6 7 8 9 10 (Yes)

4. People have told me I am charismatic.
(No) 1 2 3 4 5 6 7 8 9 10 (Yes)

Attraction power score is sum x 1 = ___

Character Power

1. I am totally honest, and people know that about me. At church, they would never question my integrity.
(No) 1 2 3 4 5 6 7 8 9 10 (Yes)

2. I always speak the truth as I know it. It can be unpleasant to be completely candid with people, but I never hide the truth just to make someone feel better or to avoid conflict.
(No) 1 2 3 4 5 6 7 8 9 10 (Yes)

3. People consider me courageous. I stand up for what I believe is right, even in the face of resistance and opposition from powerful people.
(No) 1 2 3 4 5 6 7 8 9 10 (Yes)

4. I don't preach one thing but do something different. I walk the talk, and if I make a promise, I never fail to keep it. People know they can trust me.
(No) 1 2 3 4 5 6 7 8 9 10 (Yes)

Character power score is summed x 3 = ___

To learn your personal power score, total your Knowledge, Expressive, History, Attraction, and Character Power scores: ___

Positional Power

Role Power

1. I have a leadership role in my church that gives me a great deal of authority and responsibility for the church and congregation.
	(No) 1 2 3 4 5 6 7 8 9 10 (Yes)

2. I try to influence others toward a decision rather than using my authority.
	(No) 1 2 3 4 5 6 7 8 9 10 (Yes)

3. I have been very successful in every leadership position I've had in church.
	(No) 1 2 3 4 5 6 7 8 9 10 (Yes)

4. I am one of the most senior leaders in my church.
	(No) 1 2 3 4 5 6 7 8 9 10 (Yes)

Role power score summed x 3 = ____

Resource Power

1. I control key resources that other congregants need to fulfill their roles.
	(No) 1 2 3 4 5 6 7 8 9 10 (Yes)

2. My roles include budgetary authority and oversight of other committees and units. Heads of these committees and units seek my approval.
    (No) 1 2 3 4 5 6 7 8 9 10 (Yes)

3. In my role, I manage schedules and assignments. I control access to key people.
    (No) 1 2 3 4 5 6 7 8 9 10 (Yes)

4. I own or control significant financial resources.
    (No) 1 2 3 4 5 6 7 8 9 10 (Yes)

Resource power score is summed x 1 = ___

Information Power

1. I have access to deep church information that many congregants do not have access to.
    (No) 1 2 3 4 5 6 7 8 9 10 (Yes)

2. I am highly skilled at interpreting information and presenting it in a form that others value and couldn't get from another source.
    (No) 1 2 3 4 5 6 7 8 9 10 (Yes)

3. In my church role, I manage information needed by others.
    (No 1 2 3 4 5 6 7 8 9 10 (Yes)

4. I conduct research or otherwise generate new information that is valuable and gives the church fresh insights.
    (No) 1 2 3 4 5 6 7 8 9 10 (Yes)

Information power score is summed x 1 = ___

Network Power

1. I am well-connected inside and outside my church. I know a multitude of congregants in other churches and locations.
	(No) 1 2 3 4 5 6 7 8 9 10 (Yes)

2. My network includes important people who also have large networks of their own. Through my own network and theirs, I have tremendous reach.
	(No) 1 2 3 4 5 6 7 8 9 10 (Yes)

3. I am a very active networker. I continually reach out to the people I know and maintain ties with.
	(No) 1 2 3 4 5 6 7 8 9 10 (Yes)

4. Many people want me to be part of their network because of my role, title, position, expertise, reputation, or some other reason; that makes me an attractive network member.
	(No) 1 2 3 4 5 6 7 8 9 10 (Yes)

Network power score is summed x 2 = ___

Reputation Power

1. In my church, I have an excellent reputation. Congregants hold me in high regard.
	(No) 1 2 3 4 5 6 7 8 9 10 (Yes)

2. People I just met often tell me that they've heard good things about me.
	(No) 1 2 3 4 5 6 7 8 9 10 (Yes)

3. At church, my performance has always been outstanding. I am known as a woman who gets results.
  (No) 1 2 3 4 5 6 7 8 9 10 (Yes)

4. In my church, other congregants often ask me for advice or mentoring.
  (No) 1 2 3 4 5 6 7 8 9 10 (Yes)

Reputation power score is summed x 3 = ___

To learn your positional power score, total your Role, Resource, Information, Network and Reputation Power scores: ___

Will Power

1. I know where I want to go and what I want to do in my church. I am fiercely determined to get there.
  (No) 1 2 3 4 5 6 7 8 9 10 (Yes)

2. I am not easily discouraged. Unforeseen obstacles and repeated failures could not deter me from my course.
  (No) 1 2 3 4 5 6 7 8 9 10 (Yes)

3. I am a dreamer, but I know that dreams aren't enough. I have a proven history of acting on my dreams and making them a reality.
  (No) 1 2 3 4 5 6 7 8 9 10 (Yes)

4. One of my strengths as a leader is my formidable willpower. I never waver. Nothing gets in my way.
  (No) 1 2 3 4 5 6 7 8 9 10 (Yes)

Willpower score is summed x 10 = ___

*Your Total Power Self-Assessment score is the sum of your Personal + Position + Willpower scores. Add them together:*_____

*All published parts of Power Self-Assessment, including interpretations, are adapted for a church community. Source of work is: Terry R. Bacon (2011). *The Elements of Power: Lessons on Leadership and Influence.* Atlanta, GA: American Management Association.

Interpreting Self-Assessment Score

Remember: You can't become more powerful, thereby more influential, unless you understand the elements of power. The higher your total score on this Self-Assessment, the more powerful you are in the church.

Most church women are less interested in their total Self-Assessment score, a combination of Personal, Positional, and willpower, than in identifying ways that they can improve their overall behavior. You can do this by noting which of your power sources is the weakest. Are you weaker in Personal power than in Positional power? If so, which of the five sub-areas of Personal power is lowest? Is it your character or your history? Plan how you can improve these areas.

Many women congregants aren't paid staff; consequently, their Positional power scores are low because they don't control financial resources. Don't worry about that score or waste time strategizing how to improve it. Put your energy into areas that give you a good return on your investment. Ask yourself these key questions:

1. What sources of power are most important for my role in the church? Depending on how many items you come up with, you may want to rank them from top to bottom.

2. Are you weaker in any area than you should be given your church roles? When you make your development plan, put these items near the top.

3. Look ahead—do you want another role? Which power source should you develop to prepare yourself for it?

Chapter 10

Influence in Church

To this point, *Power Up* has focused on your personal, positional, and will powers.[6] You know biblical women used power to get things done. You have concrete ideas about why power works in you and in the church. Importantly, you know your power strengths and areas that need work. Over the next few chapters, the focus is on using power. Using power is named "influence".[14]

Using power is influence!

A woman wants other church congregants to agree with her viewpoint and follow her lead. She succeeds in church when she influences others. Understanding power was Step 1. Now, the hard work of using power in the church begins. You become an influencer based on your personal, positional, and will powers.

If a woman wants to make a change in her church, she must know how to influence others.[14] Wishful thinking, degrees, and being a church member for 20 years are nice, but none of these give a woman influence in her church.

Influence is present in almost all human interactions, definitely in all communications. Many times, when a woman communicates, she attempts to change another person's mind or persuade them to think or act in a certain way. At times, women are aware that they are using influence to sway others' opinions or actions. At other times, a woman uses influence unconsciously, yet wants an explicit outcome to occur. Also, influence can produce an effect without a word being spoken. Probably, all women have been influenced by a nod, smile, or grimace.

In my years in churches, I've seen two examples of a Pastor attempting to influence congregants. At two different times, two pastors were hired to make changes in a church. They both had positional power (Pastor); however, each used different influence tactics.

In one church, the new Pastor entered the church and made no changes for a year. This Pastor took the time to assess congregants and how the church operated. She learned their values. She learned the strengths and weaknesses of congregants and the community. This knowledge allowed her to use optimal influence tactics with congregants when she initiated changes.

The second Pastor attempted to make changes in the church immediately. She didn't last a year in the job. She didn't start by assessing the situation. She didn't understand congregants. She didn't use the right influence tactics to make the changes she was hired to make. She generated hostility from congregants with the influence tactics she used. What can you learn from these two Pastors' approaches to making changes?

Influence Outcomes

Individuals attempt to influence you. Each woman is the recipient of hundreds of attempts to influence her daily.[14] If a woman responded to each attempt, she would be tossed back and forth, have no control over what she believes or wants for her life. She wouldn't know if she could safely watch a Netflix video with an X rating. The trailers are so enticing. They assure women that they will be entertained and escape life for a few hours. She could hear that watching church services online is just as meaningful as attending church services. Why brave the elements? Winter is cold, and summer is hot and humid. A woman can stay in her nightclothes if she watches the service online. Being a Sunday School participant is as meaningful as being the teacher. There's no need to do the prep work needed to teach a class. A woman can learn just as much by listening to someone else teach it.

Woman, you decide whether you will be influenced, and how much. The same goes for a target (the person you are trying to influence). They decide if and how much they will allow you to influence them.

Responding to influence is a continuum from an absolute "No" to an absolute "Yes".[14] At the center of the continuum is "Apathy," or I don't care one way or another. On the positive side are compliance, commitment, and leadership. On the negative side are skepticism, resistance, and even rebellion.

Each woman has her own goals and objectives.[14] A woman isn't attuned to what you feel or think. She is unmoved by what you want. The same is true of you. Sometimes you are unmoved by what another woman thinks or feels. You may remain as apathetic to a situation as before you heard about it. Be aware, however, in church, many women aren't in the middle (apathy) about a church issue. Usually, a woman tends (even marginally) to favor or dislike an idea.

When a woman comes with a proposal or request for help, a target is biased to respond positively or negatively. Let me give you an example in my current church. We have a mini food bank in the church parking lot. It is always available for anyone who needs food. In the church bulletin, each Sunday, there is an appeal for food with specific needs listed. Monthly, many individuals bring a bag of food to the church. Perhaps, food security was an issue for these congregants. They aren't apathetic to this issue; therefore, they comply with the church's request.

Understanding possible outcomes (positive or negative) is important, even crucial, to be a successful influencer. Today, I saw an interview with the Vice President of the U.S. He noted that sometimes he disagrees with what the President wants him to do. He tells the President his opinion, but ultimately, he says, "Yes, Sir," following the chain of command in the Executive Branch of the U.S. government.

I'm telling you this story because in church, a woman must be sure that a target has the option to respond. Before you try to influence a target—by expending a lot of thought and effort—make sure the person has an option to respond favorably or unfavorably. Perhaps money or time is tight right now; the target has no more reserves to give.

At times, influence efforts have results over time rather than immediately. For example, you ask a woman to sing in the choir. She says, "No". She tells you that she has children and can't make the Thursday evening choir. If you ask her again in several years, she may say, "Yes". Her oldest child can now watch the younger one when she is at choir practice. Alternatively, you may initiate childcare during Thursday choir practice as a way to allow more women to join the choir.

How Women Use Influence

In the 21st century, when women read the Bible, they don't expect to read about influential women. Often, women readers don't notice when a Bible woman used influence. Have you ever heard a sermon in which the Pastor said, "Notice how influential she was"? Yet, these same pastors readily identified when a Bible man influenced others, i.e., a king influenced his soldiers, a priest stirred listeners to action.

A careful analysis of 21st-century women's influence behaviors shows that women used the same influence tactics that biblical women used. Like power sources, influence tactics remain the same over time. One difference is that biblical women often applied influence tactics subtly. Have you ever wondered if women could have more leverage in churches if they were willing to be more subtle in their actions?

Social psychologists assert that subordinates know more about superiors' behavior than superiors know about subordinates' behavior.[15] Why? Subordinates spend more time observing superiors to learn how they act. Many subordinates think they need to act the same way the boss acts. Think about the truth of this social psychology finding. If you're in charge, do you really care how a subordinate behaves, even thinks? You just want them to get things done. Never forget that subordinates are watching you.

Ancient Near East society was patriarchal. Women observed men and knew which influence tactics they used. Frequently, women used the same tactics, thinking that was the right way to behave.

Twenty-first-century churchwomen observe their Pastor. The woman knows which influence strategies the Pastor uses. A woman comes to believe these influence strategies are acceptable because the Pastor uses them. Further, most congregants respond positively to the Pastor's influence tactics; therefore, they must be the right ones to use.

Congregants copy influence tactics used by the pastor.

Learn to be an Influencer

Influence effectiveness is the result of an influencer's skill at using influence tactics (detailed in subsequent chapters).[14] That means that you can learn to be an influencer in your church. Like learning any skilled craft, time and practice are required to perfect the skills of influencing.

You can learn to influence others!

Before you begin an influence attempt, ask yourself if attempting to influence others to make a change is really the best move. Right now, I am annoyed by an activity in my church. I could attempt to influence congregants or form a cabal to change these activities. But isn't it better if I pray and think before I act?

Is my preferred outcome best for the church? What would happen if what I desired occurred? Instead of wasting my influence capital and lobbying for changes that I'm not sure are the right ones, I need to pray that God will direct my heart to accept the current situation or bless any influence efforts I make.

Twenty-first-century women, who want to be optimal influencers, can begin by taking three steps:

1. <u>Assessing a situation</u>: Assessment is crucial. A woman must know what is happening in the church regarding the situation she cares about. Only after a woman understands the situation should she attempt to change it.

If a woman doesn't care about a situation, she shouldn't expend energy on it. Alternatively, if a woman cares about a situation, she should be clear about what she desires to happen, to change. The desirable outcome shouldn't be, "We need to make a change." Simply saying, "I want change" is lazy thinking.

When a churchwoman assesses a situation, she must understand power brokers. "Who are the main decision makers in this situation? Who (targets) do I need to focus my influence efforts on?" Remember, a target has his/her own perspectives and priorities. The target isn't a blank slate. Learn targets' values, i.e., what they care about or don't care about.

2. <u>Outline steps to take</u>: Social media influence is a hot topic in the first third of the 21st century. Magazines, news reports, and podcasts discuss the lives and opinions of social media influencers. Most social media influencers are women. Have women ever considered how they can use social media influence tactics to be a church influencer?

Read Table 9.1[16] carefully. In the Table are 10 steps to becoming a social media influencer. Consider what is needed to be a social media influencer, then think about how you can apply this societal trend to your behavior in church. I particularly resonate with Step 3. Develop a strategy to become a church influencer using some of this content. .

Table 9.1 Key Steps to Becoming a Social Media Influencer[16]

Step #	Topics
1	Find a niche for focus: area of interest
2	Select a platform that suits your skills
3	Develop a content strategy
4	Create quality content
5	Engage with your audience
6	Optimize outreach
7	Collaborate with others, partner
8	Be consistent & constant in content
9	Analyze your performance, use metrics.
10	Consider brand partnership, promote others' brands.

3. <u>Choose optimal influence tactics</u> to use in the situation. To be a church influencer, a woman must look honestly at herself. Which influence skills does she use? Which one does she use most often? Which influence tactic feels most familiar? Likely, she overuses this influence tactic, whether or not it's the best tactic to use.

Woman, vary your influence tactics!

At times, it's valuable for a 21st-century woman to talk to other women to learn what they think is the optimal influence strategy to use in a church situation. Is a different influence tactic needed in this situation than the one you use most often? Should you change your most-used tactics?

Anticipate pushback on many proposals and outright rejection of others. Plan counterarguments for the ones you will likely get. By anticipating pushback before it occurs, a woman can prepare responses. A woman may discover she needs to change her influence tactic; this one isn't getting the job done.

Final Thoughts

Psychologically, "power" is a strong word while "influence" seems lukewarm or namby-pamby, even negative. Nonetheless, influence evolves from power. Influence is the outcome of power.

Church women can learn to be more influential in their churches by studying the suggested steps to becoming a social media influencer. Some steps are right on; others must be adjusted for a church setting. Importantly, women who function in churches need to be willing and able to change influence tactics for a situation and for the target of their influence.

Points to Ponder

How are power and influence related?

If you decided you didn't want to influence anyone in church on a topic, would you need power?

In church, how can a woman collaborate with other congregants to accomplish a specific change objective?

Why do women need to be consistent in their behavior when attempting to influence others?

Complete the table below to contemplate a desirable change in your church.

Current Situation	Desired Situation	Power Brokers (specific names)

Chapter 11

Positive Influence Tactics

There are dozens of influence tactics. Although I am a fabulous 50+ woman, I had no idea they all existed. Most women in churches stick to using positive influence tactics. Positive influence tactics are divided into three groups. rational, emotional, and socializing.[15] Within each broad group are specific tactics. This chapter shows how biblical women used positive influence and how 21st-century women use influence in churches. Optimal ways for church women to use influence tactics are suggested.

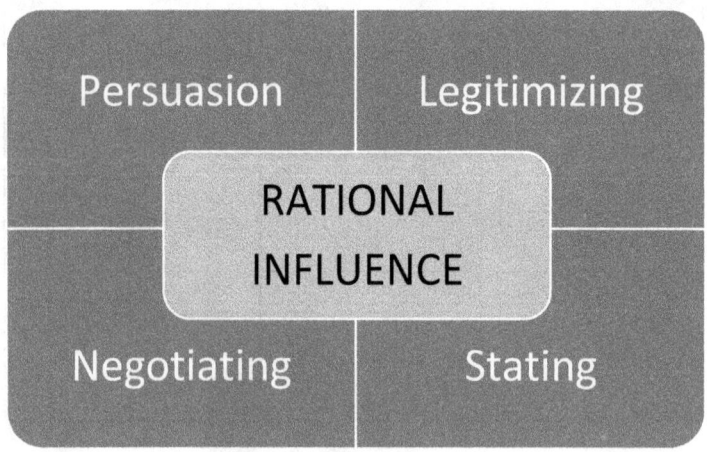

Rational Influence Model[15]

Rational Influence Tactics

Most 21st-century women think they're rational. They believe they're reasonable, logical, and sensible. When they attempt to influence others, they plan to use sensible (rational) influence tactics. Rational influence tactics are persuasion, legitimizing, negotiating (exchanging), and stating. Read through these four tactics. Think when you used each last. Did it work?

Persuasion is the number one positive influence tactic used in the world today. When Bible women used, and 21st-century women use persuasion to influence others, they use logic—or what passes for logic in their minds—to explain why others should think or act in a certain way.

Persuasion is the most used influence tactic

Often, when my husband and I leave church, I say, "We heard one side of the picture in the sermon." I want to hear both sides of a persuasive argument so that I can decide for myself. Unfortunately for me, my preference isn't the pastor's purpose in giving a Sunday sermon. The sermon's purpose is to provide guidance and instruction to congregants. That means the pastor uses persuasion in the sermon and generally doesn't give all facets of an argument.

Legitimizing: Although persuasion is the #1 influence tactic, other influence tactics are valuable in churches. In the 21st century, church leaders use God's name and quote Scripture—a rational influence tactic known as legitimizing—to coerce hearers to take what they believe is the right action. Legitimizing is an appeal to authority to influence another. In church, individuals attempt to legitimize when they say, "the Bible says," "God said," or "Pastor thinks."

Global studies showed that legitimizing is the *least effective* influence tactic for 21st-century women to use to influence others. When the Bible was written, the authority of a king or a governor was greater than today. Perhaps legitimizing was a more important influence tactic than now; however, legitimizing is still being used, particularly in churches.

Not too long ago, my husband (Bruce) contacted our church administrator, questioning a church policy. Bruce shared with the administrator that the church was taking action contrary to the denomination's bylaws. The administrator's response was, "Well, we don't really follow the bylaws." When 21st-century churchwomen use a legitimate source, such as bylaws or policy, they need to be sure that the source is adhered to in the church.

Negotiation is an exchange for cooperation. Negotiating is a *quid pro quo*; you give me x, and I will give you y. Negotiating is more effective if the negotiation is understood or implied, rather than stated openly. In the Bible, Hannah negotiated with God, praying that if God would give her a son, she would give him back to God. God caused Hannah to bear a son, Samuel. Hannah gave Samuel to God to serve in the Tabernacle at Shiloh.

Twenty-first-century church women use negotiation with other church women. An example is: If you help me with this church project that I care about, I will help you with one that you care about. These agreements between women are *quid pro quo*.

Importantly, the woman who proposes the agreement and secures the other woman's support must respond positively when she is asked for assistance. If she doesn't agree to help, most likely she won't get the needed help the next time she asks. Only rarely do women negotiate with a church pastor; generally, they follow the pastor's directions.

Stating: The final rational influence tactic, stating, is asserting what you want or believe. Stating is most effective when influencers are self-confident and state ideas or beliefs in a compelling tone. Ideally, statements are consistent with church norms. A problem with stating is that it can cause resistance, particularly if overused or used in a heavy-handed manner.

Like women in the 21st century, biblical women used stating. An example is Pilate's wife. Pilate was the Roman governor over Jerusalem. Jewish leaders wanted Pilate to condemn Jesus to be crucified. Pilate's wife sent her husband a terse message to influence his action. She stated, "Leave the innocent man alone. I suffered through a terrible nightmare about him last night" (Matthew 27:19). Unfortunately, Pilate ignored his wife's statement. He didn't allow her to influence him. Christians remember Pilate with scorn.

Emotional Influence Tactics

Strongest tactics available to church women.

Emotional influence is powerful because it targets a listener's heart.[15] Emotional appeals connect a message, goal, or project to individuals' goals and values. In targets, emotional influence tactics foster feelings of well-being, service, and a sense of belonging.

Two emotional influence tactics are 1) appeal to values and 2) role modeling. When a woman uses either of these two tactics to influence other congregants, she fits into church norms. Rightly or wrongly, men and some other women expect women to use emotional influence tactics. Common perception is that women are an emotional gender.

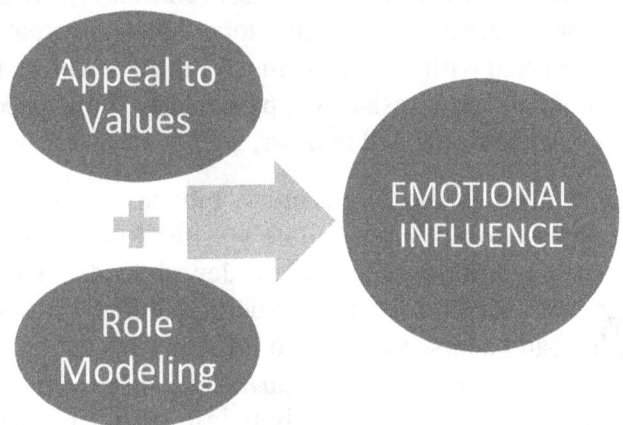

Emotional Influence Model[15]

<u>Appealing to values</u> contrasts with logical persuasion (a rational influence strategy). It is most effective when the message aligns with a target's beliefs. This tactic is ideal for gaining commitment from others for an important church project or initiative.

Today, church leaders appeal to congregants' values. Frequently, women use church doctrine, a type of shared value, to influence others to take on a project, i.e., preparing Thanksgiving baskets for low-income individuals, because Christian church doctrine teaches care for the poor and needy.

This morning on Facebook, church members received an appeal to values. The church had a leaking water pipe. Church water costs quadrupled this past month. One of our church values is that members make repairs rather than hire professionals. By the end of the day, a man volunteered to fix the water pipe.

In the first century, Peter traveled throughout Palestine, encouraging new churches. A widow, Tabitha (Dorcas), became sick and died. Hearing that Peter was in a nearby town, church leaders sent for him. When Peter arrived in Joppa, he was taken to the room where Tabitha's body lay.

Many widows stood weeping around the bed. They showed Peter the many robes and other clothing that Tabitha made for the poor. The weeping women didn't ask Peter to bring Tabitha back to life; however, their desire was consistent with Peter's beliefs about the value of good deeds in the new church. Peter prayed for Tabitha, and she was brought back to life.

No, most likely when you pray over a dead body, the individual will not come back to life. That was not the point of the Bible episode. The point was that the grieving widows appealed to Peter's Christian values, which included helping someone who aided the poor and needy, i.e., Tabatha.

Role model: In Bible times, parents, priests, Pharisees, and public figures influenced others through role modeling desirable behaviors. Today's women should be role models for how they want other women congregants to act.

The effectiveness of role modeling as an influence tactic is problematic. For role modeling to be effective, a woman must consistently practice walk her talk. When she doesn't, she undermines her credibility in church. A Church woman can't go wrong by role modeling the fruit of the Holy Spirit.

During David's reign, Israel experienced a three-year famine. God told David that the famine was the result of King Saul killing and almost decimating the Gibeonites, a non-Israelite clan who signed a peace treaty with Israel 400 years earlier. To lift the curse, the Gibeonites demanded that seven of King Saul's descendants be killed in retaliation. Two descendants were the sons of Saul and his concubine, Rizpah. Gibeonites murdered and exposed the two sons' bodies at Gibeah.

Rizpah's next action shocked all the Israelites. Rizpah took sackcloth, spread it on a rock near her sons' bodies, and sat on the cloth. By day, Rizpah kept birds off her sons' bodies. At night, she fought off wild animals. Rizpah remained at the site of the exposed bodies for at least six to eight months, including during the heat of the long Israelite summer.

King David learned of Rizpah's action. He saw how she role modeled care of loved ones' bodies. He gathered the bones of the dead and buried them along with those of King Saul and Jonathan. Rizpah's actions are one of the Bible's greatest stories of a mother's love.

Social Influence Tactics

Women socialize with each other in church. When a churchwoman wants to influence another, she frequently uses social influence tactics. There are four social influence tactics: socializing, appealing to relationships, consulting, and alliance building.[15] At times, these influence strategies are ethical and done with integrity. At other times, a churchwoman's attempts at social influence are selfish, even immoral. Probably, no woman has at all times used influence beneficially, even in church.

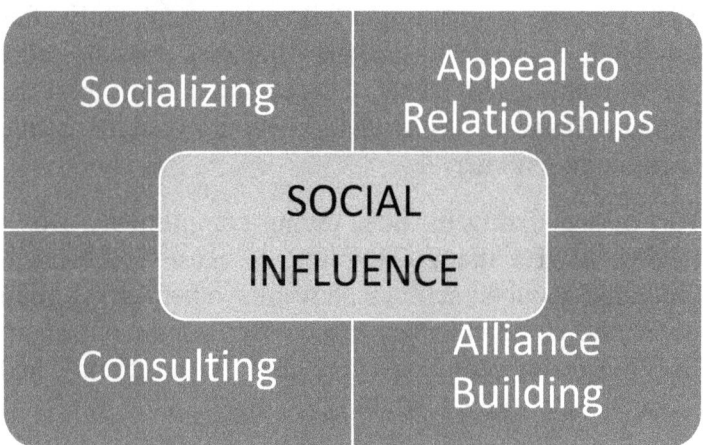

Social Influence Model[15]

Socializing is an excellent way to influence others. When socializing, women learn and adopt the beliefs, values, behaviors, and norms of a church. A woman adapts her behavior to fit with those of the church, or she decides to look for another church. This church doesn't fit her beliefs or values.

Generally, Bible women appeared open and friendly as they found common ground. In 21st-century churches, women are open as they get to know each other through the give-and-take of conversations. In my church, congregants arrive about 10 minutes early and visit with each other. Often, they hang around after service. They spend that time talking with old friends and meeting new attendees. It's a time to show caring and interest in each other.

While socializing, a woman observes how another woman behaves in multiple situations, i.e., in casual conversations, in Sunday school classes, helping with VBS, and when preparing a fellowship meal. Only after a woman observes how another behaves does she trust the woman, or maybe she decides she doesn't trust the woman. If she trusts a woman, she will spend more time socializing with her.

Part of socializing includes giving compliments. Don't neglect to give them. Compliments cause a woman to feel good about herself, which results in her feeling good about the complementor. If you like something about her, a woman concludes you must be discerning and someone she wants to know.

> *Make a person feel good—*
> *she's more likely to socialize with you.*

Alternatively, if the number of compliments is overdone, the complementor gets a reputation for being fawning. I like to compliment individuals, but check that I don't overdo it. What about you? Are you able to use compliments wisely as you socialize in your church?

Appeal to Relationship: When a woman attempts to influence another by appealing to a relationship with her, two factors are crucial: 1) the strength of the relationship and 2) at times, the length of it. Women in superficial or new relationships have little or no influence over each other. Only after a relationship has been in place for some time can a woman influence another. Rarely can you walk up to a woman you've not spoken to previously and ask for a favor, even a church-related favor.

Ideally, a 21st-century woman investigates a target's perspective before trying to influence her. Maybe the target woman already believes or feels the same as the influencer. In that case, the influencer needn't expend any effort convincing her of her perspective. The challenge is when the target feels or believes differently from the influencer. Having a relationship with another woman allows a woman to tailor her approach so it resonates with the target's values and beliefs.

Alternatively, a woman may decide that attempting to influence the other woman isn't a good use of time and energy. For example, the influencer decides the target woman is set in her ways and viewpoints and is unwilling to change her mind.

Salome is thought to be James and John's mother, thus Jesus' aunt. Salome traveled with and helped to fund Jesus' ministry. Salome believed she knew Jesus well enough and long enough that she could influence him by appealing to their relationship (Matthew 20:20-28).

Salome approached Jesus and asked him for a "favor." The favor wasn't for herself, but for her two sons. She wanted Jesus to grant that James and John sit on Jesus' right and left hands in his kingdom. Jesus refused Salome's request, saying that he didn't have the power to grant it. Only God decides who sits at Jesus' right and left hands in heaven.

Reread the dynamics of Salome's request to Jesus and his refusal. Note that Jesus gave a reason for his refusal. Using Jesus' model, a churchwoman needs to give a reason if she declines a request.

<u>Consulting</u> means discussing, asking, checking, and conferring. Often, the influencer/consultant asks the target relevant questions to get her involved in the situation. Thus, targets feel valued and invested in ownership of the decision and committed to its outcome.

Once committed to an outcome, a woman rarely seeks additional information; however, if new information comes her way, she doesn't ignore it. She considers it; thus, her perspective may waver or change altogether. A woman who uses consulting as an influence tactic ideally checks back to see if her target's opinion remains the same.

A closer look at consulting shows it's a type of collaboration, a type of partnership, even teamwork. During the consulting/collaborating process, it's easy for a woman to influence another in the give and take of conversation. When Bible women collaborated, usually more information was available. A more comprehensive solution resulted. The same is true in 21st-century churches.

Consulting works well in almost all societies, ancient and contemporary. A challenge in today's churches is diverse population groups in the congregation. This diversity must be factored into an influence process, particularly consulting/collaborating.

Congregants in my church are chiefly non-Hispanic Whites, but some are Hispanics, Blacks, and Asians. We are a cross-section of income and professional levels. Several attendees are developmentally challenged. Some congregants were immersed in the drug culture for a time.

Consulting assumes a target cares about the topic.

Women, we must learn how to consult in churches with diverse groups!!! The U.S. is a plural society; hopefully, churches are too. The first step when interacting with a congregant whose characteristics are substantially different from your own is to listen and respect what the other says. Definitely talk to God about how to work with diverse individuals. Follow Jesus' direction—love our neighbor (church congregation) as ourselves.

Alliance Building: In churches, much alliance building refers to partnering with other churches, ministries, or community organizations to achieve shared goals. Often, shared goals focus on outreach, social impact, or advocacy. A network of supportive and collective action is created to amplify churches' resources and influence beyond individual congregations.

The above paragraph isn't the focus for women building alliances in their church. In their own churches, alliance-building moves beyond a woman being the sole influencer. The alliance builder gains the cooperation of other women and groups and uses them to help her influence others.

An example of a failed alliance is: A woman in a church believed that she and her Pastor shared the same belief on an issue the church wrestled with. Discussion between the two supported her belief. Later, one of the Pastor's sermons averred a different belief. When questioned, the Pastor responded that her new position evolved from a closer Bible reading.

The woman had a crisis of confidence in her Pastor. She no longer saw the Pastor as trustworthy or as an ally. She could have concluded that the alliance was broken on one issue only and proceeded in the relationship because their alliance was strong in other areas.

Candidly, that didn't happen. The woman was shaken. She wondered if the Pastor would change her mind on other church positions and activities. That's the problem with alliance-building with other women. Women, including yourself, can change their minds. An alliance can fracture.

One of the best alliance builders in the Bible was an Israelite slave girl (2 Kings 5:1-19). Naaman was the valued head of Aram's armies. Naaman had leprosy. Naaman captured a young Israelite girl and gave her to his wife as a servant. The Israelite girl told her mistress that if Naaman went to God's prophet (Elisha) in Samaria, the prophet could cure him.

The girl didn't try to influence Naaman directly. Instead, she built an alliance with her mistress, who told her husband the girl's words. Naaman told the King of Aram. The King of Aram sent a letter and Naaman to Israel's king, "With this letter I am sending with my servant Naaman so that you may cure him of his leprosy"

(2 Kings 5:6). The Israelite slave girl started the alliance-building process, which ended with Naaman cured of leprosy.

Have you ever wondered what happened to this Israelite slave girl? Most likely, her status in Naaman's home improved because he was healed. But what would have happened to the girl if Naaman refused to follow Elisha's instructions and bathe in the Jordan River? What would have been her treatment had Naaman returned to Aram with the same skin condition as he left with? Likely, her status would have worsened.

Final Thoughts

In the Bible and in the 21st century, power precedes influence. Women can learn influence tactics, but first, they must know what tactics are used and acceptable in their church. Ideally, women approach objectives by thinking through how they can go about achieving them. Which positive influence should they use? Ideally, a woman never forgets who she represents. No, it's not a country nor a political party. It is God.

Positive influence tactics fall into three categories: rational, emotional, and social. Persuasion is the number one rational influence technique used in churches. Legitimizing, also a rational influence technique, is largely unsuccessful.

Emotional influence tactics are the strongest tactics available to church women. Emotional influence tactics include 1) appeal to a woman's values and 2) a role model of what is good and right.

Social influence tactics depend on the behaviors of both influencers and targets. More than with rational and emotional influence tactics, social influence tactics depend on the integrity of both.

Points to Ponder

Evaluate your ability to influence others in church. Why do your influence tactics work? Why don't they work? Are you a successful influencer more often than a failed influencer?

Which rational influence tactic do you use most often? Why do you use it?

Describe a time you attempted to influence someone by referring to God or to Scripture. Did you succeed? Speculate why you succeeded or why you failed.

Why are emotional influence tactics so powerful? How are they emotional?

Think about and/or share a time when you influenced someone by your actions (role model). Are there times when you wished that you hadn't exhibited that action, i.e., didn't role model that action?

Rate from top to bottom, which social influence tactics you use most often in your various church roles,

How would you rate/evaluate alliance-building as an influence tactic? What are the steps in building an alliance in your church?

When is alliance-building worth the effort/not worth the effort at church?

Chapter 12

Negative Manoeuvres

Be honest. Women can be negative. Even if a woman isn't an overall negative person, sometimes she uses negative influence tactics. If she's a Christian, why would a woman do something negative? The answer is—because negative influence tactics can get results.

Like positive influence tactics, negative ones depend on a woman having power in her sphere, i.e., the church. Psychologists identified four negative influence tactics: avoiding, manipulating, intimidating, and threatening.[15] These influence tactics are named "negative" because they take away another person's legitimate right to say "No."

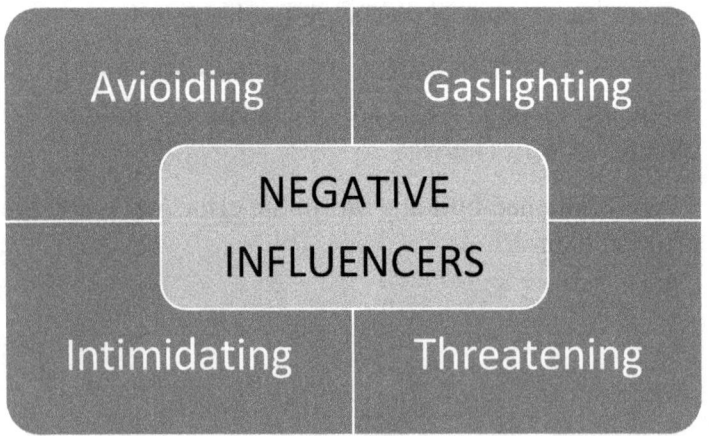

Types of Negative Influencers[15]

They pressure individuals to do something or agree to something they don't want to do. Negative influence tactics can force targets to act when they would rather not act. Negative influence harms targets' thoughts, behavior, and well-being. Negative influence can create unhealthy habits in targets, can cause them to make poor choices, and ultimately reduce their happiness.

Is negative influence permeating your church? Is it present in you? Maybe!!! This section describes and gives examples of Bible women who used negative influence tactics. The chapter suggests four ways for women to defang the power of negative influence.

<u>Avoidance</u> is the most used dark-side tactic. Avoidance involves choosing not to address disagreements or tensions. Avoidance occurs when a woman refuses to acknowledge or take responsibility for feelings or actions.

Bible stories showed that avoidance was a common tactic used among ancient Israelite women. Perhaps Bible women avoided conflict situations because they knew they saw and interacted with each other daily. Old Testament Israelite society wasn't mobile. Ancient Israelite women lived their entire lives in the same town. They wanted to keep their relationships smooth.

In an Old Testament episode, no one won because Princess Tamar avoided telling her father, King David, that Prince Amnon raped her, his half-sister (2 Samuel 13:1-22). Following the rape, Tamar went to her brother's, Prince Absalom, home and told him what happened. Subsequently, Tamar lived with her brother, rather than return to her mother's house.

By Tamar's action, she avoided telling her father what happened. At the same time, Tamar influenced her brother, Prince Absalom, to obtain justice for her. Prince Absalom killed Prince Amnon in retaliation for raping Tamar. Subsequently, King David exiled Absalom for killing his oldest son and heir. Years later, when Prince Absalom returned from exile, he initiated a rebellion against his father.

Princess Tamar's choice to avoid telling her father what happened led to Prince Ammon's death and ultimately to a civil war in Israel, which ended with Absalom's death. This episode shows that avoidance can be dangerous.

Several Sundays ago in church, I shared with two women friends that I was going to give a party for a church couple who planned to get married. One friend asserted vigorously that she wasn't attending. I had no idea what to say, so I said, "You have a right not to attend." I avoided addressing her distress/concerns. I avoided conflict. Perhaps I lacked confidence in my ability to deal with a dispute while retaining a friendship.

Avoidance is not a personality trait.
It's behavior.

Often, churchwomen avoid confrontation by word choice. They avoid challenging language, such as in my example above. In church, women may avoid disagreeing with each other by saying nothing. Another way women avoid conflict is by changing the subject, particularly if a topic is sensitive. At times, women remove themselves physically from a conversation, i.e., they excuse themselves.

If an issue doesn't matter to a woman, conflict avoidance is a good option. Avoiding situations, positions, etc., that mattered little, saves a woman's energy. Possibly, they save a woman's reputation in church. If it does matter, then a discussion is needed to identify the cause of the conflict and to explore how the conflict can be resolved.

Before ending this section on avoidance, a cautionary note for church women: when possible, avoid opposition, disagreement, and confrontation with your Pastor; otherwise, you will end up in the one-down position at the episode's end. Congregants rarely come out ahead in conflict with a pastor. Pastors have much power and influence in a church.

Manipulation is disguising intentions or intentionally withholding information that another person needs to make the right decision. A manipulator maneuvers the target to do or say what the manipulator desires.

Manipulation includes lies, deceit, hoaxes, swindles, persistence, cons, and coercion (subtle or obvious). If you're not sure what these behaviors look like, watch the cable news shows. Using questions, commentators guide (manipulate) guests to give desired answers. Talking heads (commentators) give only part of a story; thus, they manipulate viewers into believing something that isn't true.

Bible women manipulated others. They were manipulated by others. Rachel was a manipulator throughout her life (Genesis chapter 29 through 31). In one Bible episode, Rachel manipulated both her father and husband. When Jacob and family left Paddan Aram,

Rachel stole her father's (Laban) household images (gods). Rachel's husband, Jacob, knew nothing of the theft. When Laban caught up with Jacob to take back his household gods, Jacob denied having them. Jacob permitted Laban to search his tents for the images.

When Laban entered Rachel's tent, Rachel was seated on a camel saddle under which the household images were hidden. Rachel told Laban that she couldn't rise because she had her menses. By not rising, Rachel prevented Laban from searching in or under the saddle. Rachel's action deceived and manipulated both her father and husband.

A 21st-century word for manipulation is gaslighting. Gaslighting causes a person to question their own reality. It's emotional abuse. Here are ways gaslighting (manipulation) works:

- The abuser denies facts, feelings, or the victim's perception of reality: "You're overreacting". "You're remembering what I said wrongly".

- The abuser tries to make victims doubt their own instincts and self-esteem.

- The abuser tries to shift the focus from their abusive behavior to the victim's perceived instability.

Women in church aren't immune to gaslighting and manipulating others. Likewise, they aren't immune to being manipulated

Intimidation: Normally, women think of intimidation as causing someone to feel timid in the face of real or implied threats; yet intimidation isn't always the result of a person's actions. For example, a woman can feel fear/intimidation at the prospect of speaking in front of a group or being in an unfamiliar setting. Intimidation can include feeling an overwhelming respect for a person or place. Unfortunately, intimidation can silence a message God gave a woman. Fear becomes god rather than God's direction.

Intimidation can be mental forcing.

Intimidation is the preferred tactic of bullies. When bullies deliberately intimidate others, they impose themselves and their ideas on them. Bullies intrude or force themselves into an individual's personal, physical, and mental space. Intimidating individuals can be loud, overbearing, or abrasive. Read the following Bible story of a slave girl in ancient Philippi who intimidated early missionaries.

The slave girl told fortunes because an evil spirit lived inside her. She followed Paul and other missionaries for several days, always loudly stating the same words: "These men are servants of the Most High God, who are telling you the way to be saved" (Acts 16:17). What the girl said was true, but the girl's loud voice and repetitive message harassed missionaries and intimidated listeners. Using a loud voice, the Philippian slave forced herself on the missionaries and listeners.

Is it ever okay for a woman to gaslight another in church?

In 21st-century churches, women encounter intimidation. Also, a churchwoman can be intimidating even when she doesn't want to be. Sometimes other women ask about a target's job, what her spouse does, or where she lives. Then, the asker and possibly the hearers are intimidated by the target's response.

As I wrote this chapter, I came across a new term, "spiritual intimidation." When Pastors and church leaders demand absolute submission to their own authority and/or unquestioning loyalty to them, they can intimidate congregants. Women, many of whom have been socialized to be submissive, are ready victims of spiritual intimidation.

Decades ago, I told my Pastor that he was spiritually abusing me. I would have said spiritually intimidating if that word had been used back then. He commented that I overreacted to the situation. He denied my feelings. Perhaps he was right, and I was wrong. Yet, I felt pressured to believe something that I really didn't believe. Spiritual intimidation isn't a new phenomenon.

Some Pastors enforce legalistic rules. At times, these Pastors' actions are intimidating. Peter gave these instructions to church elders, including Pastors:

> Care for the flock that God has entrusted to you. Watch over it willingly, not grudgingly—not for what you can get out of it, but because you are eager to serve the Lord. Don't lord it over the people assigned to your care but lead them by your own good example (1 Peter 5:2-3).

<u>Threats</u>: When we think of "threats," we envision tyrants who threaten friends and foes alike to get compliance. But threats can come from Pastors, elders, and leaders in the church, including women leaders.

A threat expresses intent to inflict damage. The damage need not be physical. It can be to a church woman's credibility or reputation. Generally, the threat goes like this: Do what I want you to, or I will punish you and/or those you love. If tyrants use and follow up on threats enough times, they simply give an order, and recipients obey. The "or I will" no longer needs to be said. Listeners know a threat is implied and forthcoming if compliance doesn't occur. Often, women who are threatened feel insecure or anxious, sometimes angry.

The Christian church has a history of threats. By the late third century, women were threatened with excommunication if they attempted to lead Christian church congregations or offer communion. Individuals could be excommunicated if they believed something different from the orthodox position of the Church. After the Reformation, beliefs that were mainstream in some churches were grounds for excommunication in others.

Pastors frighten congregants in sermons when they outline the sure outcome for individuals who aren't redeemed by Christ. This sermon threat is different from a threat designed as social influence from peer to peer pr maybe pastor to parishioner.

Threatening behavior among congregants is rarely open. A subtle threat can be as simple as ignoring a woman's input. Doing so is threatening her with exclusion. Often, threats are in the eyes of the beholder.

Threats can occur without words!

Threats are most meaningful when they come from someone we care about. In the Bible, Rachel threatened her husband, Jacob. Rachel was Jacob's favorite wife;

Jacob loved her deeply. He spent most nights with Rachel and had intercourse with her; nonetheless, Rachel didn't become pregnant. The couple was childless. Rachel told Jacob, "Give me children, or I shall die!" (Genesis 30:1). Jacob felt threatened by Rachel's outburst. He didn't want to lose his beloved Rachel. Jacob pushed back at Rachel, angrily saying that he wasn't God to ensure that she had children. Jacob was frustrated, even hurt, by Rachel's threat.

Rejecting Negative Influence

Women don't have to fall for others' negative influence. Below are four ways to deal with a situation where another individual uses negative influence:

1. Be aware of what's happening around you! Do you walk into church on Sunday morning or Wednesday Bible study, breeze past everyone without a smile or a hello? Or perhaps worse yet, give that fake smile of yours? Do you see—actually see—the women in the foyer, talking to each other, smiling, even greeting you?

If this is how you approach church, you are ripe to be a victim of negative influence. Your actions say you don't care about the women; consequently, why should they care about you? You have no concerns about using negative influence tactics, i.e., avoidance, on them. Why should they have any qualms about using negative influence tactics on you?

You don't have to accept all people in your church as friends; however, ideally, you treat all of them courteously, even pray for them. Importantly, you can decide not to respond to their negative influences. Decide you will not play in that playground of negativity while still being an active member of a church. Think!

Be aware! Engage! Pray that God will give you a heart of flesh rather than a heart of stone.

2. Make effective decisions about individuals and environments you expose yourself to, even in church. Being a participative woman doesn't mean you have to attend every event. My church is having a dessert party to fund youth activities. I'm trying to lose weight; therefore, I won't attend the dessert party. It's okay to say that you have other plans without giving specific details.

3. Know what's important to you and what's holding you back.

Identify what you care about now, realizing that what you care about changes over time. Pray that God will stir your heart to care about what he wants you to care about. You want to be sure your thinking and actions are consistent with God's.

Take your time and pray before you decide on important issues. Search the Scriptures. Ask God to give you his perspective on a topic. If you spend the time clarifying what you believe and assuring it's consistent with what God teaches/ordains, you won't succumb to negative influence tactics.

4. Look for positive influencers in your church and interact with them.

Identifying positive influencers in a church isn't easy. An individual can be a positive influence in one area but not another. An example is a person who continually prays for ill and infirm members but doesn't care about Christian education. Possibly, God gave the woman a soft heart for ill congregants. If God gave you the same concern or ministry, seek this woman out and interact with her. It's okay that you aren't involved in all church ministries.

Vary your church friends to learn the breadth and depth of each. At the same time, avoid being part of a cabal of negative influencers.

Final Thoughts

Influence tactics are designed to be used to promote unity among fellow congregants and help congregants come together; to copy a trite and often used saying, "to be all that we can be" as a church.

Negative influence tactics are rarely rational. They hurt others when used inside churches. Negativity can be daunting. Remember the verse in Galatians that reminds us not to grow weary in doing good (Galatians 6:9). It can be applied to women in churches—don't be weary (drained) and default to negative influence tactics to get what you want. Spend time contemplating how not to succumb to negative feelings and influence tactics. Remember, when you are tired, you are often negative.

Points to Ponder

Why do you think that "avoidance" is the most used dark side influence tactic?

Which negative influence tactic do you use most often in church?

Is it acceptable for a Christian woman to use negative influence tactics on individuals in the community or home but not in the church?

If a woman is aware that she is being manipulated, is it okay to go ahead and manipulate her? What if she is unaware? Is it okay to manipulate her?

Remember Jesus' story of the persistent widow who eventually obtained her desired result from the corrupt judge (Luke 18:1-8)? Did she intimidate the judge? Jesus commended her actions. Is persistence the same as intimidation? If not, how do the two differ?

Ending Up

Initially, it seemed unrealistic to go to the Bible to find information on women's power and influence. Then, I considered the words of King Solomon (Ecclesiastes 1:9):

What has been done will be done again.

The power and influence of women in the 21st century is an echo of women's behavior through the millennia. The behaviors of women in today's church aren't unique. The power and influence requirements for 21st-century women were present in ancient Israel and in the early Christian church.

When I studied the power and influence of Bible women, my first realization was that some Bible women were young. Esther was around 15-20 years old when she became Queen of Persia. Mary, the mother of Jesus, was probably younger than 15 years old when an angel asked her to be the mother of the Messiah.

From my perspective as a middle-aged woman, I asked myself, "How could God put these young women in this position?" Their brains weren't fully developed. Neither were their thought processes; consequently, their beliefs and behaviors weren't mature. Did they really know what they were doing or agreeing to do?

I don't know the answer to my questions, but I do know that God's thoughts are far above mine. My role is to trust God without having all the answers. Last Saturday, I attended a teaching conference at church. The teaching leader said that maturing Christians were in tension between asking God legitimate questions—even having legitimate doubts—and having our thoughts informed by what Scripture tells us. I strive for a biblical perspective as I question and receive answers from God on the power and influence of biblical women. I feel tension viewing women's roles and behavior in society and the church.

Immediately before Jesus was taken up into heaven, he told his disciples that "You will receive power when the Holy Spirit comes on you" (Acts 1:8). Jesus was speaking to both men and women. Both in the Christian church of the first century and in the 21st century, women are given power when they receive the Holy Spirit. The Spirit is the same Spirit for men and women. The Holy Spirit is the same spirit that women received millennia ago.

References

1. Barna. (2025). New research in church attendance: Decline of women and rise of men. www.barna.com.

2. Hallowell, Bill. (August 2022) Why churches allow women pastors? www.faithwire.com.

3. The Center for American Progress. (n.d.). The economic state of single mothers. www.Americanprogress.org.

4. Beasley, Brett. (n.d.). Four ways to use your power ethically. Center for Ethical Leadership. University of Notre Dame. www.ethicalleadership.nd.edu.

5. National Association of Evangelicals. (n.d.). Code of Ethics for Congregations & Their Leadership Team. www.nae.org.

6. Bacon, Terry R. (2011). *The Elements of Power, Lessons on Leadership and Influence.* Atlanta, GA: American Management Association.

7. Blank, Avery. (2017). Ways leaders use silence to increase their power (and you can, too). *ForbesWomen.* www.forbes.com.

8. Humphrey, Judith. (2018). Six verbs that make you sound weak (no matter your job title). *Fast Company.* www.fastcompany.com.

9. Rock, David, and Dixit, Jay. (January 2023). Are our brains wired to quiet quit? Harvard Business Review. www.hhb.org.

10. Forster, Greg. (2013). The radical Christian approach to poverty and riches. The Gospel Coalition. www.thegospelcoalition.org.

11. Whitman, Walt. (n.d.). Favorites. www.azquotes.com/quotes/56404.

12. McNair, Rod. (2012). Willpower. *Tomorrow's World*. www.tomorrowsworld.org.

13. McGonigal, Kelly. (2012). *The willpower instinct*. New York: Penguin Group.

14. Bacon, Terry R. (2012). *Elements of Influence, The Art of Getting Others to Follow Your Lead*. Atlanta, GA: American Management Association.

15. Weir, Kristen. (2017). Power play. American Psychological Association. www.apa.org.

16. Dharmalingam, Abiram. (August 2025). Steps to being a social media influencer. NM Marketing Solutions. www.nmmarketingsolutions.in.

Models and Tables

Model/Table	Page
Diagram of Bacon's Model of Power	31
Sources of Personal Power	32, 51
Sources of Positional Power	33, 69
Composition of Willpower	34, 99
Table 9.1 Key Steps to Becoming a Social Media Influencer	128
Rational Influence Model	131
Emotional Influence Model	135
Social Influence Model	138
Types of Negative Influence	147

Author Information

Dr. Carolyn A. Roth

Carolyn is a spiritual woman who believes in God the Father, God the Son, and God the Holy Spirit. She believes that words in the Bible are God-inspired. She writes books for the laity rather than clergy or theologians. Many of her books are designed as Bible studies.

Dr. Carolyn A. Roth has advanced degrees in psychology. She was a former Army nurse. She taught for 25 years in universities. Her last full-time position was as a Distinguished Professor. Carolyn is ordained as a Protestant minister.

Carolyn is eager to hear your questions and comments. For more information on her and her other publications, use this address to contact Carolyn: carolyn.roth@ymail.com. Her books are available in paperback, audio, and electronic format at: https://www.amazon.com/author/carolynaroth.

Another Read

Level Up, Time to mature your faith

Christians toil to live a Jesus-centered life. This book is for those Christians who want help with day-to-day living. The book's overall purpose is to show 21st-century Christians how to level up their Christian walk by applying Bible stories.

The book has two specific objectives. The first is to take a deep dive into Bible episodes. Bible stories show characters' efforts to walk with God. Some efforts succeeded. Some failed. All teach us. God expects Christians to know and learn from Bible stories. That's why they're in the Bible.

The book's second objective is to apply the outcomes of Bible episodes to our efforts to live a more successful Christian life in the 21st century. Specific suggestions for success are suggested if you find yourself in a similar situation as one of these biblical characters.

Leveling up our Christian walk doesn't sound all that hard. Possibly, you asked, "Do I really need this book? How is it different from a thousand other books on the market?"

The book is different because it integrates Bible (the Christian's self-help book) instruction with the latest information on how to make behavioral changes. Further, instructions are documented with biblical references, lots and lots of Bible references.

The book engages and stimulates your thinking. Chapters incorporate thought-provoking questions throughout. Questions require you to take an in-depth look at how you live your life. You decide if you want to go in your current direction. Alternatively, is it time to make a directional change? Do you need a course correction? I've made mine. I've already gone through the process outlined in this book once. It wasn't quick or easy. Maybe I'll go through it a few more times.

Each chapter's final page is "Delving Deeper." Delving Deeper is filled with questions that encourage you to take a deeper dive into Holy Scripture. Then, deliberate on what you believe and, importantly, why you believe it. Questions are ideally suited for individuals or groups

www.ingramcontent.com/pod-product-compliance
Lightning Source LLC
LaVergne TN
LVHW020347260326
834688LV00045B/1583